FLORENCE'S GLASSWARE Pattern IDENTIFICATION GUIDE

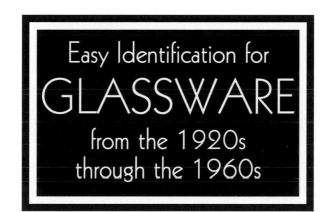

Easy Identification for
GLASSWARE
from the 1920s
through the 1960s

COLLECTOR BOOKS

A Division of Schroeder Publishing Co., Inc

Searching for a Publisher?

We are always looking for knowledgeable people considered to be experts within their fields. If you feel that there is a real need for a book on your collectible subject and have a large comprehensive collection, contact Collector Books.

On the Cover:

Upper left: Tinkerbell pattern by Morgantown

Lower right: La Fontaine pattern by Tiffin

Bottom: Formal Chintz pattern by Heisey

Ice Bucket in background: Diane pattern by Cambridge

Cover design by Beth Summers
Book design by Holly C. Long

Collector Books
P.O. Box 3009
Paducah, Kentucky 42002 – 3009

Gene Florence
P.O. Box 22185   P.O. Box 64
Lexington, KY 40522   Astatula, FL 34705

Copyright © 1998 by Gene Florence

Printed in the U.S.A. by Image Graphics, Paducah, KY

INTRODUCTION

Over the years, the publisher and I have discussed photographing strictly a patterns identification book, batting around various ideas. It was all simply discussion until last spring when he suddenly decided he wanted me to do one! He presented his core idea. I thought immediately that it would be a good place to show pieces not identified in my other books which consistently generate letters and photos in my mail. Cathy, my wife, thought it ought to include collectible items presently languishing in the markets because no one recognizes what they are. In seconds, we went from research mostly completed to mountains of it to do. I, also, found myself agreeing to a couple of other books; and suddenly, my ensuing year leaped from peaceful to chaotic in the blink of an eye.

Then, in June, came health problems in the form of diabetes, and my 18-hour day energy level dropped to five hours tops! Thus, getting this book out on schedule has been due in very large part to hours and hours of work done over the last eight months by my wife. She helped search markets for pieces to picture, spent hours documenting them, and packaged box upon box of glass to send to the photographer. She sifted the stacks of completed photographs into manageable, named order for layout once that point was reached; and she expended tons of midnight oil amid stacks of books and before the computer trying to dig out facts about colors, items manufactured, and dates, typing them onto computer printouts for use by the editor and staff, all of whom were "pitching in" to make this book reality.

Cathy experienced frustration in the market place, either not finding a pattern she particularly wanted, or finding a piece priced too exorbitantly to justify its expense against its collectible value for the book. She ran into researcher's woes by finding different names, dates, and companies of manufacture for the same items. Sometimes, there was wonderfully precise catalog data; most times, there was not. We've consulted the works of other authorities in their fields (see Bibliography) and collectors whom we deemed knowledgeable. On occasion, we've resorted to counting on our fingers the number of items or colors we've seen over our 30 years in the business. Cathy acknowledges that she did not find at least two sources of reference for every piece shown and that the items (made) references are certainly not to be considered as written in stone. However, in the limited format set for the book, we have tried to present as complete a sketch as possible of the various patterns of glass represented here. Keep in mind, our main objective was to show a clear picture of these various patterns of glass!

If you have additional information regarding any pattern shown, please feel free to share it. Should the book reach a second printing, you may be certain I'll pass the information along! There's still much to be found and enjoyed! Happy collecting!

PATTERN NAME: ADAM
Company: Jeannette Glass Company
Years: 1932 – 1934
Colors: pink, green, crystal, yellow, delphite blue
Items: 37

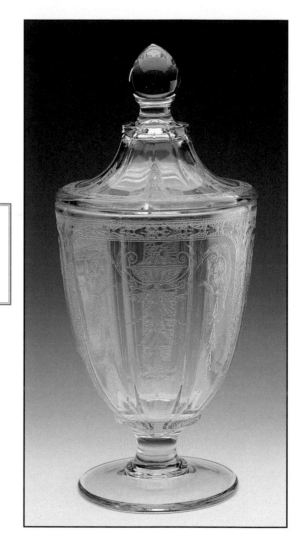

PATTERN NAME: ADAMS #100
Company: The Cambridge Glass Company
Years: ca. 1921
Colors: crystal
Items: 36+

PATTERN NAME: ADAM
Company: Tiffin Glass Company
Years: 1929 – 1934
Colors: crystal, rose, green
Items: 45

PATTERN NAME: ALICE
Company: Anchor Hocking Glass Company
Years: 1945 – 1949
Colors: jade-ite, vitrock, vitrock with
          red or blue trim
Items: 3

PATTERN NAME: ALPINE/CAPRICE
Company: The Cambridge Glass Company
Years: 1915 – 1986
Colors: blue or crystal with satin
Items: 75+

PATTERN NAME: AMERICAN,
              LINE #2056
Company: Fostoria Glass
          Company
Years: 1915 – 1986
Colors: crystal, some amber,
          blue, green, yellow,
          pink tinting to purple
          in the late 1920s, red in
          1980s; red and crystal
          by Lancaster Colony
          for Dalzell Viking
Items: 320+

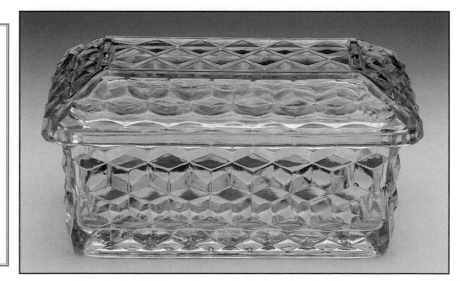

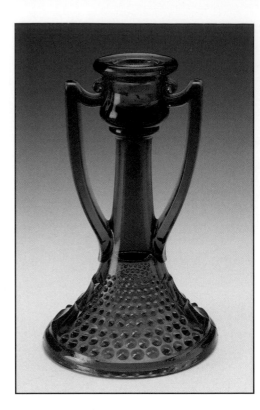

PATTERN NAME: AMERICAN PIONEER
Company: Liberty Works Glass Company
Years: 1931 – 1934
Colors: pink, green, amber, crystal
Items: 21

PATTERN NAME: AMERICAN SWEETHEART
Company: MacBeth-Evans Glass Company
Years: 1930 – 1936
Colors: pink, monax, red, blue, cremax, color-
           trimmed monax
Items: 33

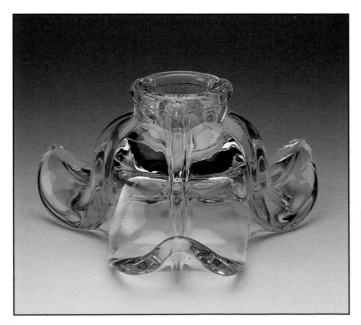

PATTERN NAME: AMERICAN WAY #71
Company: The Duncan & Miller Glass Company
Years: 1940s
Colors: crystal
Items: 26+

PATTERN NAME: ANCESTRAL #14
Company: New Martinsville Glass
            Manufacturing Company
Years: 1940s – 1950s
Colors: crystal, colors
Items: 27

PATTERN NAME: ANNIVERSARY
Company: Jeannette Glass Company
Years: 1947 – 1949, late 1960s – 1970s
Colors: pink, crystal, shell pink, iridescent
Items: 29

PATTERN NAME: APPLE BLOSSOM, LINE #3400
Company: The Cambridge Glass Company
Years: 1930s
Colors: blue, pink, light and dark green, yellow, crystal,
            amber, heatherbloom, black with white gold
Items: 100+

PATTERN NAME: AQUA CREST
Company: Fenton Art Glass Company
Years: ca. 1940
Colors: white with aqua
Items: 24+

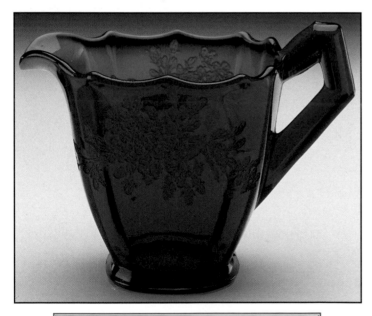

PATTERN NAME: ARDITH, LINE #411
Company: Paden City Glass
Manufacturing Company
Years: 1920s – 1930s
Colors: royal blue, yellow, crystal
Items: 10+

PATTERN NAME: ARCADIAN
Company: Tiffin Glass Company
Years: 1918 – 1935
Colors: crystal with gold, amber
Items: 14

PATTERN NAME: ARGUS
Company: Fostoria Glass Company
Years: 1963 – 1982
Colors: crystal, olive green,
            cobalt, red, gray
Items: 14

PATTERN NAME: ARTURA, LINE #608
Company: Indiana Glass Company
Years: 1930s
Colors: crystal, pink, green
Items: 7

PATTERN NAME: ASTER, LINE #13628
Company: Tiffin Glass Company
Years: 1915 – 1936
Colors: crystal
Items: 12+

PATTERN NAME: AUNT POLLY
Company: U.S.Glass Company
Years: 1920s
Colors: blue, green, iridescent
Items: 21

PATTERN NAME: AURORA
Company: Hazel-Atlas Glass Company
Years: 1930s
Colors: cobalt, pink, green, crystal
Items: 7

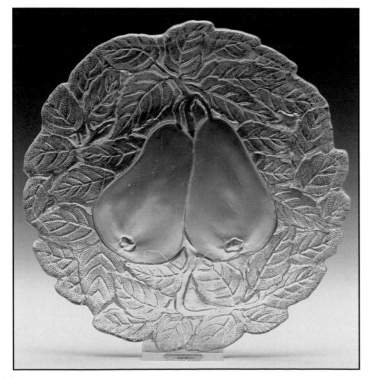

PATTERN NAME: AVOCADO
Company: Indiana Glass Company
Years: 1923 – 1933; remade 1974…
Colors: pink, green, crystal, white
Items: 16

PATTERN NAME: AZURITE SWIRL
Company: Anchor Hocking Glass Company
Years: 1950s
Colors: opaque blue
Items: 13

PATTERN NAME: BADEN #777
Company: Morgantown Glass Company
Years: 1930s
Colors: crystal, crystal with black
Items: 5+

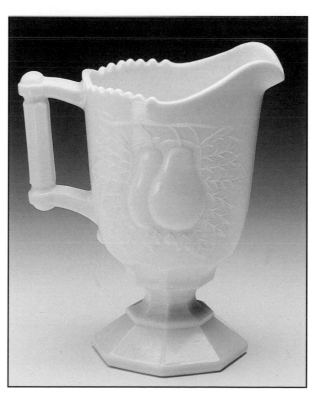

PATTERN NAME: BALTIMORE PEAR,
               SHELL PINK
Company: Jeannette Glass Company
Years: late 1940s – 1970s
Colors: shell pink, crystal
Items: 12+

PATTERN NAME: BANDED FLUTE, #150
Company: A. H. Heisey & Company
Years: 1907 – 1932
Colors: crystal
Items: 100+

PATTERN NAME: BAROQUE #2496
Company: Fostoria Glass Company
Years: 1936 – 1966
Colors: crystal, azure, gold tint, yellow,
           green, pink, red, blue
Items: 68

PATTERN NAME: BEADED BLOCK
Company: Imperial Glass Company
Years: 1927 – 1930s
Colors: pink, green, crystal, blue, yellow,
           iridescent, amber, red, opalescent,
           white
Items: 21+

PATTERN NAME: BEADED EDGE, PATTERN #22
Company: Westmoreland Glass Company
Years: 1930s – 1950s
Colors: milk glass, milk glass with decoration
Items: 21+

PATTERN NAME: BIG TOP PEANUT BUTTER
Company: Unknown
Years: 1950s
Colors: crystal
Items: 7

PATTERN NAME: BLACK FOREST
Company: Paden City Glass
    Manufacturing Company
Years: 1929 – 1930s
Colors: amber, blue, black with
    gold, crystal, green,
    pink, red, cobalt
Items: 45+

PATTERN NAME: BLOCK OPTIC
Company: Hocking Glass Company
Years: 1929 – 1933
Colors: green, pink, yellow, crystal,
           amber, blue
Items: 56+

PATTERN NAME: BLUE MOSAIC
Company: Anchor Hocking Glass Company
Years: 1966 – 1969
Colors: white with blue decals
Items: 12

PATTERN NAME: BO PEEP, DESIGN #854
Company: The Monongah Glass Company
Years: 1930
Colors: pink, crystal with green
Items: 13+

PATTERN NAME: BOWKNOT
Company: Unknown
Years: 1920s?
Colors: green
Items: 7

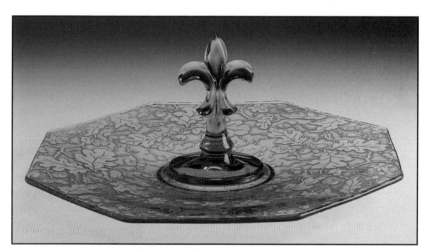

PATTERN NAME: BROCADE #290, OAK LEAF
Company: Fostoria Glass Company
Years: 1928 – 1931
Colors: crystal, green, pink, blue
Items: 60+

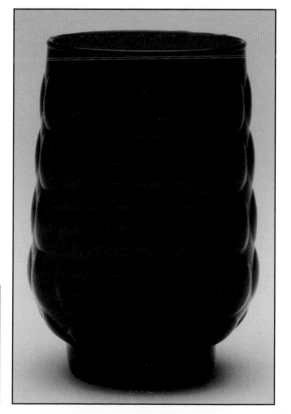

PATTERN NAME: BUBBLE, HOCKING
Company: Anchor Hocking Glass Company
Years: 1941 – 1968
Colors: pink, blue, forest green, ruby red,
           crystal, amber, peach lustre, jade-ite
Items: 32

PATTERN NAME: BUTTERFLY,
            DECORATION 797
Company: Lotus Glass Company
Years: 1925 – 1932
Colors: yellow
Items: 18

PATTERN NAME: BUTTERCUP,
            ETCH #340
Company: Fostoria Glass Company
Years: 1941 – 1960
Colors: crystal
Items: 60+

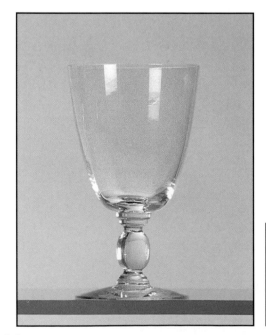

PATTERN NAME: CABOCHON
Company: A. H. Heisey & Company
Years: 1950 – 1957
Colors: amber, crystal, dawn
Items: 37

PATTERN NAME: CADENA
Company: Tiffin Glass Company
Years: 1932 – 1934
Colors: crystal, yellow, pink
Items: 32+

PATTERN NAME: CAMELIA
Company: Jeannette Glass Company
Years: 1947 – 1951
Colors: crystal, crystal with gold trim
Items: 9+

PATTERN NAME: CAMELIA, ETCH #344
Company: Fostoria Glass Company
Years: 1952 – 1965
Colors: crystal
Items: 88

PATTERN NAME: CAMEO
Company: Hocking Glass Company
Years: 1930 – 1934
Colors: green, yellow, pink, crystal, crystal
          with silver trim
Items: 68

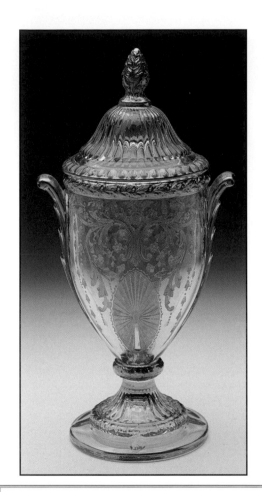

PATTERN NAME: CANDLELIGHT
Company: Cambridge Glass Company
Years: 1940s – early 1950s
Colors: crystal, Crown Tuscan with
          gold decoration
Items: 88+

PATTERN NAME: CANDLEWICK, LINE 400
Company: Imperial Glass Company
Years: 1936 – 1984
Colors: crystal, blue, pink, yellow,
          black, cobalt blue, green, slag,
          ruby
Items: 365+

PATTERN NAME: CANDLEWICK
MALLARD CUT
Company: Imperial Glass Company
Years: 1940s
Colors: crystal
Items: 40+

PATTERN NAME: CANTERBURY #115
Company: The Duncan & Miller Glass Company
Years: 1938 – 1956
Colors: crystal, blue, red, pink, yellow,
chartreuse and opalescent colors
Items: 150+

PATTERN NAME: CANTERBURY, ETCH #31
JANICE BLANK, LINE #4500
Company: New Martinsville Glass Company
Years: 1932 – 1944
Colors: crystal
Items: 10+

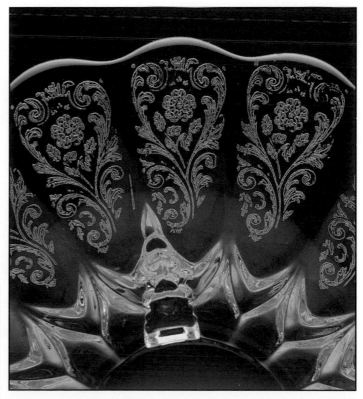

PATTERN NAME: CAPE COD
Company: Imperial Glass Company
Years: 1932 – 1984
Colors: amber, crystal, blue, cobalt
           blue, red, green, black, milk
           glass, pink
Items: 150+

PATTERN NAME: CAPRI
Company: Hazel-Atlas Glass
           Company
Years: 1960s
Colors: azure blue
Items: 66+

PATTERN NAME: CAPRICE
Company: Cambridge Glass Company
Years: 1936 – 1958
Colors: crystal, blue, white,
           amber, pink, emerald
           green, cobalt blue,
           amethyst
Items: 275+

PATTERN NAME: CARIBBEAN, LINE 112
Company: The Duncan & Miller
              Glass Company
Years: 1935 – 1955
Colors: blue, crystal, amber, red
Items: 82+

PATTERN NAME: CASCADE, LINE 4000
Company: The Cambridge Glass Company
Years: 1947 – 1956
Colors: crystal, emerald green, milk
        glass, gold
Items: 47

PATTERN NAME: CASCADE
Company: Tiffin Glass Company
Years: 1935 – 1940s
Colors: crystal, blue, yellow,
        satin
Items: 60+

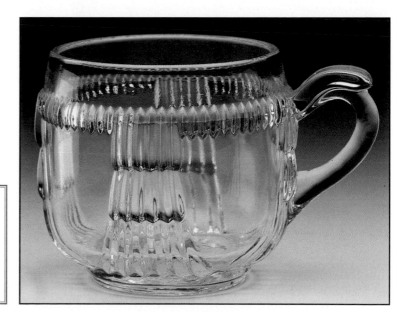

PATTERN NAME: CATHAY #811
Company: Morgantown Glass Company
Years: 1918 – 1920s
Colors: pink, crystal, green
Items: 15+

PATTERN NAME: CATHEDRAL #1413
Company: A.H. Heisey & Company
Years: 1932 – 1944
Colors: crystal, green, pink, yellow,
          cobalt, alexandrite
Items: 3

PATTERN NAME: CENTURY, LINE #2630
Company: Fostoria Glass Company
Years: 1949 – 1982
Colors: crystal, pink
Items: 74

PATTERN NAME: CERISE
Company: Tiffin Glass Company
Years: 1940s – 1950s
Colors: crystal
Items: 50+

PATTERN NAME: CHANTILLY
Company: Cambridge Glass Company
Years: 1940s – 1950s
Colors: crystal, black with gold,
          Crown Tuscan with gold
Items: 106+

PATTERN NAME: CHARM
Company: Anchor Hocking Glass Company
Years: 1950 – 1956
Colors: azur-ite, forest green, ivory, jade-
          ite, pink, royal ruby
Items: 11

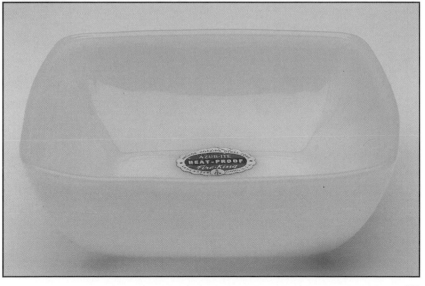

PATTERN NAME: CHARTER OAK, LINE 3362
Company: A.H. Heisey & Company
Years: 1926 – 1935
Colors: crystal, pink, green, marigold,
          Hawthorne
Items: 22

PATTERN NAME: CHECKERBOARD
          & WINDMILL
Company: Unknown
Years: ca. 1930s
Colors: green, crystal, iridescent
Items: 7

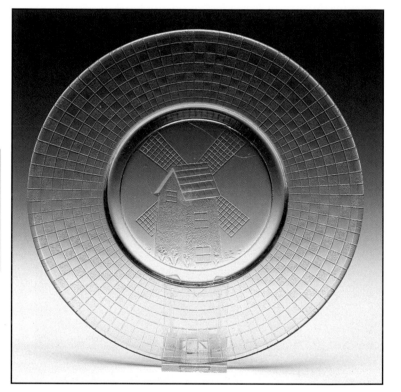

PATTERN NAME: CHEROKEE ROSE
Company: Tiffin Glass Company
Years: 1940s – 1950s
Colors: crystal
Items: 50+

PATTERN NAME: CHERRYBERRY
Company: U.S. Glass Company
Years: ca. 1930s
Colors: pink, green, crystal, iridescent
Items: 20

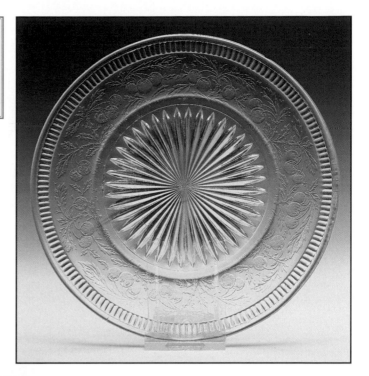

PATTERN NAME: CHERRY BLOSSOM
Company: Jeannette Glass Company
Years: 1930 – 1939
Colors: pink, green, delphite, crystal,
jade-ite, red, yellow
Items: 43

PATTERN NAME: CHEVALIER
Company: Paden City Glass
Manufacturing Company,
Canton Glass Works
Years: 1935 – 1950s
Colors: crystal, amber, forest
green, pink, cobalt, ruby
Items: 18

PATTERN NAME: CHEVRON
Company: Hazel-Atlas Glass Company
Years: ca. 1930s
Colors: cobalt, pink, crystal
Items: 3

PATTERN NAME: CHINEX CLASSIC
Company: MacBeth-Evans
Glass Company
Years: 1930s – 1940s
Colors: ivory, ivory with decals
Items: 16

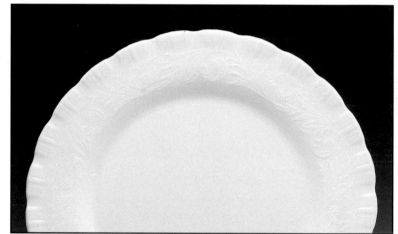

PATTERN NAME: CHINTZ, ETCH 338
Company: Fostoria Glass Company
Years: 1940 – 1977
Colors: crystal, red with gold
Items: 73

PATTERN NAME: CHINTZ 1401
Company: A.H. Heisey & Company
Years: 1931 – 1938
Colors: crystal, yellow, alexandrite
Items: 44+

PATTERN NAME: CHRISTMAS CANDY #624
Company: Indiana Glass Company
Years: 1937 – ca. 1950s
Colors: crystal, teal
Items: 13

PATTERN NAME: CIRCLE
Company: Hocking Glass Company
Years: 1929 – 1930s
Colors: crystal, green, pink
Items: 24

PATTERN NAME: CLASSIC
Company: Tiffin Glass Company
Years: 1913 – 1936
Colors: crystal, pink with crystal, pink with green, pink
Items: 32+

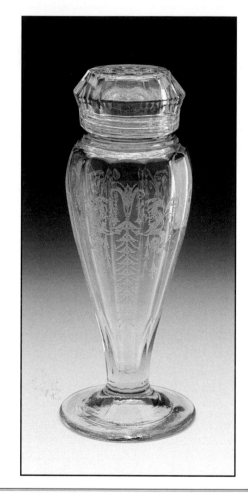

PATTERN NAME: CLOVERLEAF
Company: Hazel Atlas Glass Company
Years: ca. 1930 – 1935
Colors: black, crystal, green, pink, yellow
Items: 30+

PATTERN NAME: CLEO
Company: Cambridge Glass Company
Years: ca. 1921 – 1930s
Colors: amber, blue, crystal, green, pink, yellow
Items: 125+

PATTERN NAME: COIN, LINE #1372
Company: Fostoria Glass Company
Years: 1958 – 1982
Colors: amber, blue, crystal,
green, olive, red
Items: 53

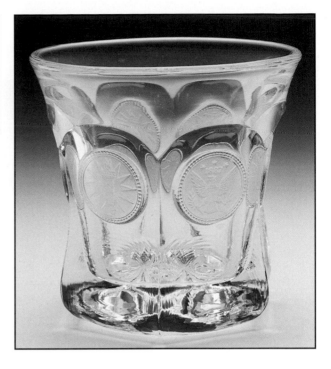

PATTERN NAME: COLONIAL BLOCK
Company: Hazel-Atlas Glass Company
Years: early 1930s
Colors: green, crystal, black, pink,
cobalt blue, white in 1950s
Items: 20

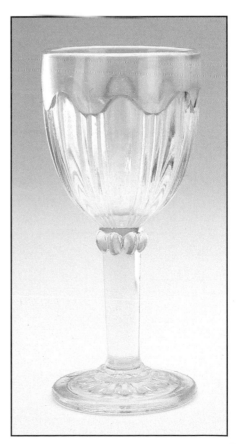

PATTERN NAME: COLONIAL "KNIFE & FORK"
Company: Hocking Glass Company
Years: 1934 – 1936
Colors: pink, green, crystal, white
Items: 40

PATTERN NAME: COLONIAL #351,
                 PRISCILLA
Company: A.H. Heisey & Company
Years: 1905 – 1930
Colors: crystal
Items: 130+

PATTERN NAME: COLONIAL FLUTED
Company: Federal Glass Company
Years: 1928 – 1933
Colors: crystal, green
Items: 12

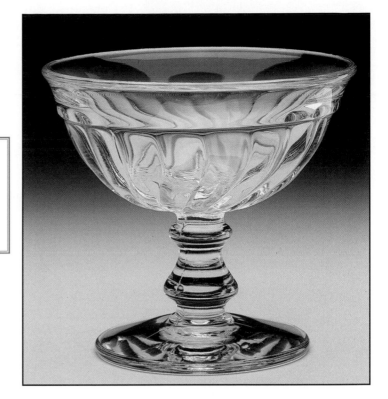

PATTERN NAME: COLONY, 2412
Company: Fostoria Glass Company
Years: 1938 – 1983
Colors: crystal, blue, green,
           white, amber, red, yellow
Items: 95+

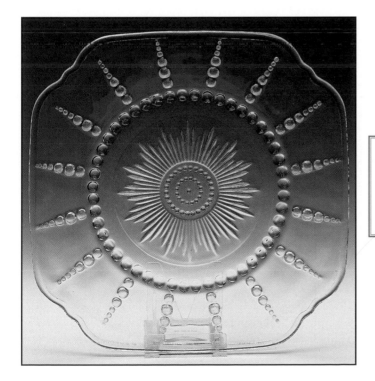

PATTERN NAME: COLUMBIA
Company: Federal Glass Company
Years: 1938 – 1942
Colors: crystal, pink, satin crystal
Items: 15

PATTERN NAME: CONTOUR PATTERN #2666
Company: Fostoria Glass Company
Years: 1955 – 1970s
Colors: crystal, pink
Items: 56

PATTERN NAME: CORINTHIAN
Company: Imperial Glass Company
Years: 1937
Colors: crystal
Items: 16

PATTERN NAME: CORONATION
Company: Hocking Glass Company
Years: 1936 – 1940
Colors: pink, green, crystal,
           royal ruby
Items: 20+

PATTERN NAME: CORONET #15360
Company: Tiffin Glass Company
Years: 1936 – 1940
Colors: crystal
Items: 40+

PATTERN NAME: CORSAGE, ETCH #325
Company: Fostoria Glass Company
Years: 1935 – 1960
Colors: crystal
Items: 63

PATTERN NAME: CRACKLE
Company: McKee Glass Company
Years: mid-1920s
Colors: crystal
Items: 8+

PATTERN NAME: CREMAX "PIE CRUST"
Company: Pyrex, division of Corning (Canada)
Years: 1930s – 1940s
Colors: cremax, white with colored trim and decals, blue
Items: 12

PATTERN NAME: CREMAX "BORDETTE"
Company: MacBeth-Evans Glass Company
Years: ca. 1940 – 1941
Colors: blue, yellow, pink, or green border trim on cremax
Items: 12

PATTERN NAME: CROCHETED CRYSTAL
Company: Imperial Glass Company
Years: 1943 – 1950s
Colors: crystal
Items: 38+

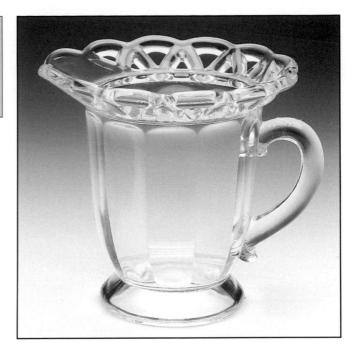

PATTERN NAME: CROESUS (722), 3500 STEMLINE
Company: Cambridge Glass Company
Years: 1938 – 1956
Colors: crystal
Items: 15

PATTERN NAME: CROW'S FOOT, #412
Company: Paden City Glass
Manufacturing Company
Years: 1920s – 1930s
Colors: crystal, black, red, amber,
amethyst, pink, white, yellow
Items: 50+

PATTERN NAME: CROW'S FOOT,
#890
Company: Paden City Glass
Manufacturing Company
Years: 1930s
Colors: crystal with silver
overlay, red, blue
Items: 20+

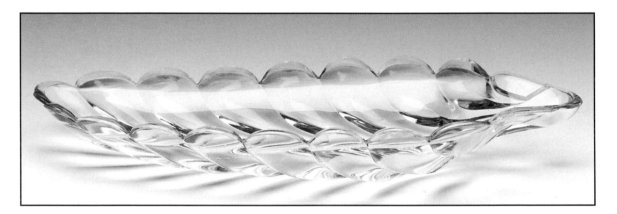

PATTERN NAME: CRYSTALINA, LINE #334
Company: Hobbs/U.S. Glass Company
Years: 1890 – 1920s
Colors: crystal with red or amber
Items: 17

PATTERN NAME: CRYSTOLITE,
BLANK #1503
Company: A.H. Heisey & Company
Years: ca. 1938
Colors: crystal, zircon, sahara,
amber
Items: 114+

PATTERN NAME: CUBE
Company: Jeannette Glass Company
Years: 1929 – 1933
Colors: amber, blue, crystal, green, pink, white, teal, yellow
Items: 23

PATTERN NAME: CUPID
Company: Paden City Glass Manufacturing Company
Years: ca. 1930s
Colors: crystal, amber, black, blue, green, pink, yellow
Items: 30+

PATTERN NAME: DAFFODIL
Company: The Cambridge Glass Company
Years: 1950s
Colors: crystal, crystal with gold
Items: 50+

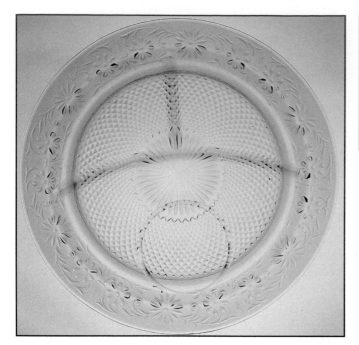

PATTERN NAME: DAISY
Company: Indiana Glass Company
Years: 1933 – 1940;
          1960s – 1980s
Colors: crystal, amber, white, fired
          red; avocado
Items: 22

PATTERN NAME: "DANCE OF THE NUDES"
                DANCING NYMPH
Company: Consolidated Glass
          Company
Years: 1920s
Colors: crystal, satin crystal, pink,
          green, white, brown, blue
Items: 15+

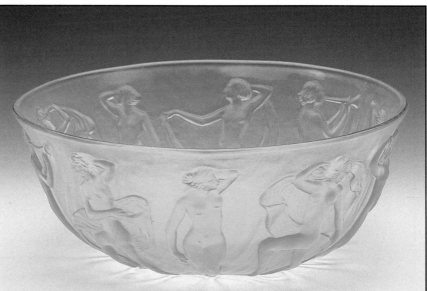

PATTERN NAME: DECAGON
Company: Cambridge Glass Company
Years: 1930s – 1940s
Colors: emerald, pink, red, blue,
          amber, black, crystal
Items: 70+

PATTERN NAME: DECAGON, LINE 1011
Company: Westmoreland Glass Company
Years: 1929 – 1933
Colors: various with trims
Items: 19

PATTERN NAME: DECORATION #5
Company: Tiffin Glass Company
Years: 1924 – 1939
Colors: opaque crystal
Items: 5+

PATTERN NAME: DEERWOOD
Company: U.S. Glass Company
Years: 1920s – 1930s
Colors: amber, green, pink,
                 black with gold, crystal
Items: 30+

PATTERN NAME: DELLA ROBBIA, #1053
Company: Westmoreland Glass
          Company
Years: 1920s – 1940s
Colors: crystal with colors, milk
          glass, opaque blue
Items: 55

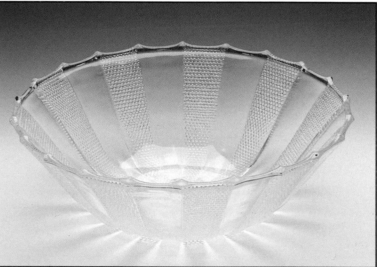

PATTERN NAME: DEWDROP
Company: Jeannette Glass Company
Years: 1953 – 1956
Colors: crystal, iridescent
Items: 18

PATTERN NAME: DIAMOND POINT
Company: Indiana Glass Company
Years: late 1950s – 1980s
Colors: crystal with red, crystal,
          amber, black, blue, green
Items: 50+

PATTERN NAME: DIAMOND QUILTED
Company: Imperial Glass Company
Years: late 1920s – early 1930s
Colors: pink, blue, green, crystal,
           black, red, amber
Items: 40+

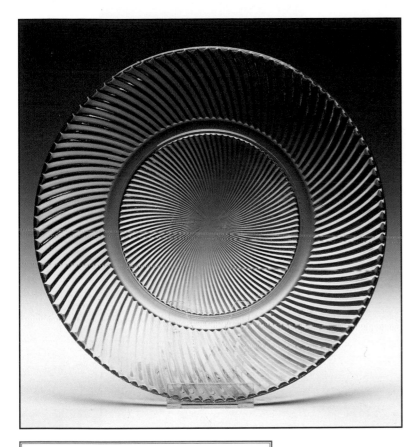

PATTERN NAME: DIANA
Company: Federal Glass Company
Years: 1937 – 1941
Colors: pink, amber, crystal
Items: 20

PATTERN NAME: DIANA #442
Company: A.H. Heisey & Company
Years: 1925 – 1937
Colors: crystal, crystal with green
Items: 22

PATTERN NAME: DIANE
Company: Cambridge Glass Company
Years: 1934 – 1950s
Colors: crystal, pink, yellow, blue, emerald, amber, Crown Tuscan, heatherbloom
Items: 130+

PATTERN NAME: DOGWOOD
Company: MacBeth-Evans Glass Company
Years: 1930 – 1934
Colors: pink, green, crystal, monax, cremax, yellow
Items: 27

PATTERN NAME: DIMITY #17501
Company: Tiffin Glass Company
Years: 1950s
Colors: crystal
Items: 10+

PATTERN NAME: DORIC
Company: Jeannette Glass Company
Years: 1935 – 1938
Colors: pink, green, delphite, ultra-marine, yellow
Items: 34

PATTERN NAME: DORIC & PANSY
Company: Jeannette Glass Company
Years: 1937 – 1938
Colors: ultra-marine, crystal, pink
Items: 22

PATTERN NAME: EARLY AMERICAN PRESCUT
Company: Anchor Hocking Glass Company
Years: 1960 – 1987; 1 vase 1998
Colors: crystal; ruby red; blue; gold; amber, avocado, and red tints
Items: 63+

PATTERN NAME: ELAINE
Company: Cambridge Glass Company
Years: 1934 – 1950s
Colors: crystal, black with gold,
           Crown Tuscan with gold
Items: 108+

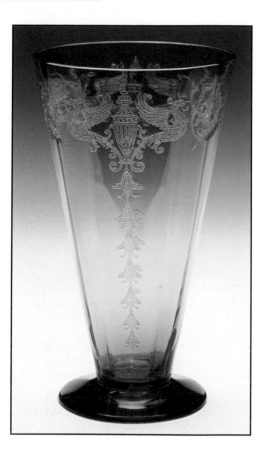

PATTERN NAME: EL DORADO
Company: Tiffin Glass Company
Years: 1920 – 1929
Colors: amber, crystal
Items: 27+

PATTERN NAME: ELIZABETH, ETCH
              #757
Company: Morgantown Glass Works
Years: ca. 1930s
Colors: azure blue, crystal
Items: 7+

PATTERN NAME: EMERALD CREST
Company: Fenton Art Glass Company
Years: 1949 – 1955
Colors: white with green
Items: 43+

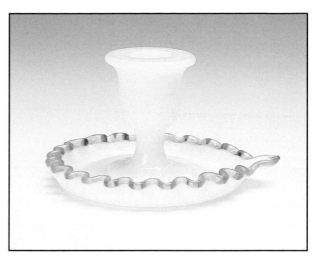

PATTERN NAME: EMERALD GLO
Company: Paden City Glass
Manufacturing Company
Years: 1940s – 1950s
Colors: emerald
Items: 30+

PATTERN NAME: EMERALD GLO WITH
STAR CUT
Company: Fenton Art Glass Company
Years: 1940s – 1950s
Colors: emerald
Items: 20+

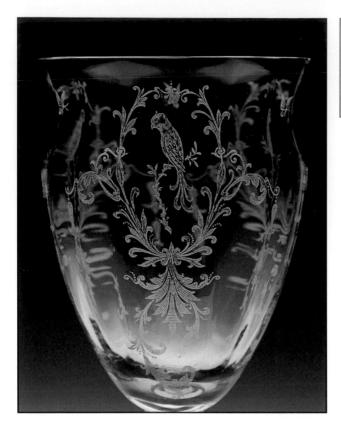

PATTERN NAME: EMPIRE
Company: Tiffin Glass Company
Years: 1922 – 1931
Colors: crystal, pink, green
Items: 18

PATTERN NAME: EMPRESS BLANK #1401
Company: A.H. Heisey & Company
Years: 1932 – 1934
Colors: pink, yellow, green, cobalt, alexandrite, tangerine
Items: 100

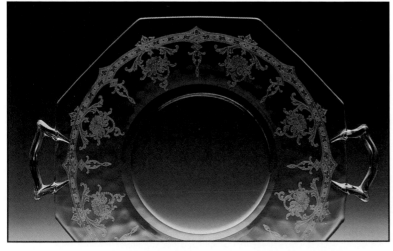

PATTERN NAME: EMPRESS, ETCH #447
Company: A.H. Heisey & Company
Years: ca. 1926
Colors: crystal, pink, green, yellow
Items: 59

PATTERN NAME: ENGLISH HOBNAIL, LINE 555
Company: Westmoreland Glass Company
Years: 1920s – 1983
Colors: amber, crystal, pink, turquoise, cobalt blue, green, black, red
Items: 175+

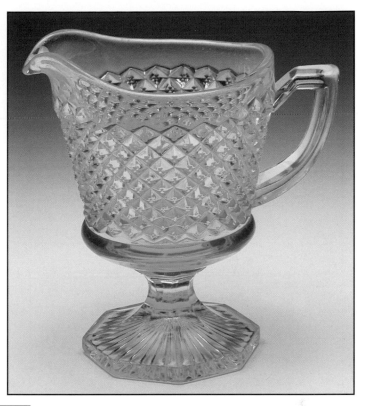

PATTERN NAME: EPIC, #119
Company: Viking Glass Company
Years: ca. 1957
Colors: amethyst
Items: 70+

PATTERN NAME: ETCH #606, TWIST STEM 117
Company: Tiffin Glass Company
Years: 1930s
Colors: crystal
Items: 7+

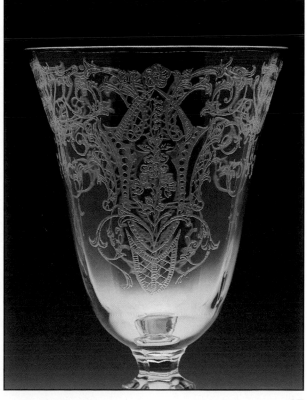

PATTERN NAME: ETCH #704
(WINDOWS BORDER)
Company: The Cambridge
Glass Company
Years: 1925 – ca. 1938
Colors: pink, green, crystal
Items: 50+

PATTERN NAME: ETCH #724 WITH
CHRYSANTHEMUM
Company: The Cambridge
Glass Company
Years: 1930s
Colors: green
Items: 6

PATTERN NAME: ETCH #732 (MAJESTIC
SANS RIM)
Company: The Cambridge Glass Company
Years: 1930s
Colors: amber
Items: 26

PATTERN NAME: EVERGLADE
Company: The Cambridge
           Glass Company,
           Imperial Glass Company
Years: 1930s – 1940s; 1970s
Colors: amber, crystal, emerald,
           milk glass, blue, red;
           white carnival
Items: 38

PATTERN NAME: FAIRFAX, #2375
Company: Fostoria Glass Company
Years: 1927 – 1944
Colors: blue, azure, orchid, amber, pink,
           green, yellow, red, black, white
Items: 92

PATTERN NAME: FAIRMONT, #2718
Company: Fostoria Glass Company
Years: 1940s
Colors: amber, blue, crystal,
           green
Items: 6

PATTERN NAME: FANCY COLONIAL #582
Company: Imperial Glass Company
Years: 1914 – 1920s
Colors: crystal, pink, iridized, blue, green
Items: 80+

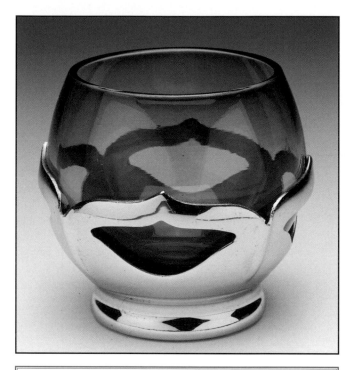

PATTERN NAME: FARBERWARE
Company: Farber Glass Company,
         The Cambridge Glass Company
Years: 1940s – 1950s
Colors: amber, emerald, amethyst, cobalt
        blue, crystal, red, crystal with cut
Items: 100+

PATTERN NAME: FESTIVE
Company: Duncan & Miller Glass Company
Years: late 1940s
Colors: yellow, blue/green
Items: 15+

PATTERN NAME: FESTOON OPTIC
Company: Tiffin Glass Company
Years: 1930 – 1935
Colors: crystal, crystal with black, yellow
Items: 9

PATTERN NAME: FINE RIB
Company: Hazel-Atlas Glass Company
Years: 1930s
Colors: pink, green, crystal, blue
Items: 5

PATTERN NAME: FIRE-KING OVEN GLASS
Company: Anchor Hocking Glass Company
Years: 1940 – 1950s
Colors: sapphire blue, crystal, ivory, jade-ite
Items: 55+

PATTERN NAME: FIRST LOVE
Company: Duncan & Miller Glass Company
Years: 1937– 1950s
Colors: crystal
Items: 200+

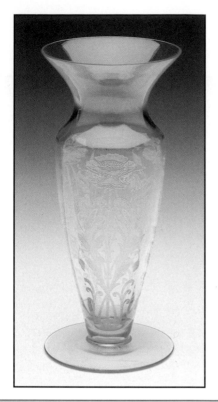

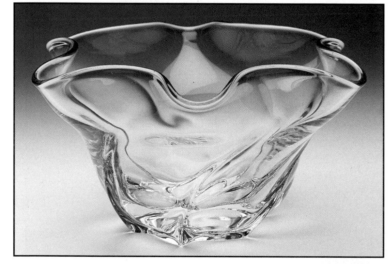

PATTERN NAME: FLANDERS
Company: Tiffin Glass Company
Years: 1910 – 1930s
Colors: crystal, pink, yellow, green
Items: 50+

PATTERN NAME: FLAIR
Company: Duncan & Miller Glass Company
Years: late 1940s
Colors: crystal
Items: 49+

PATTERN NAME: FLEURETTE
Company: Anchor Hocking Glass Company
Years: 1958 – 1961
Colors: white with decal
Items: 15

PATTERN NAME: FLORAGOLD
Company: Jeannette Glass Company
Years: 1950s – 1960s
Colors: iridescent, shell pink, ice blue, crystal
Items: 35

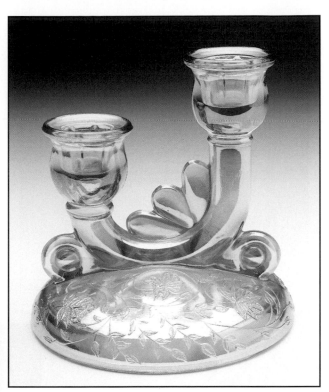

PATTERN NAME: FLORAL
Company: Jeannette Glass Company
Years: 1930 – 1937
Colors: pink, green, delphite, jade-ite, crystal, amber, red, black
Items: 49

PATTERN NAME: FLORAL & DIAMOND BAND
Company: U. S. Glass Company
Years: late 1920s
Colors: pink, green, iridescent, black, crystal
Items: 15

FLORAL & DIAMOND BAND

PATTERN NAME: FLORENTINE #1
Company: Hazel-Atlas Glass Company
Years: 1932 – 1934
Colors: pink, green, crystal, yellow,
           cobalt
Items: 35

PATTERN NAME: FLORENTINE #2
Company: Hazel-Atlas
          Glass Company
Years: 1932 – 1936
Colors: pink, green, crystal,
          cobalt, amber, blue
Items: 49

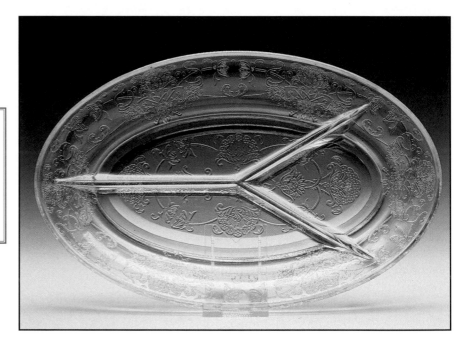

PATTERN NAME: FLORENTINE, ETCH #29,
              4400 – TEARDROP BLANK
Company: New Martinsville Glass
          Manufacturing Company,
          Viking Glass Company
Years: 1940s
Colors: crystal
Items: 27

PATTERN NAME: FLOWER GARDEN WITH BUTTERFLIES
Company: U.S. Glass Company
Years: 1920s
Colors: crystal, pink, blue, amber, green, teal, black
Items: 31

PATTERN NAME: FLYING NUN, #15011
Company: Tiffin Glass Company
Years: 1930s
Colors: crystal with green
Items: 10+

PATTERN NAME: FOREST GREEN
Company: Anchor Hocking Glass Company
Years: 1950 – 1965
Colors: green
Items: 50+

PATTERN NAME: FOREST GREEN CHARM
Company: Anchor Hocking Glass Company
Years: 1950 – 1954
Colors: green
Items: 11

PATTERN NAME: FORGET ME NOT,
        FLANGE LINE
Company: Westmoreland
        Glass Company
Years: 1930s
Colors: various applied
Items: many

PATTERN NAME: FORMAL CHINTZ,
        #450½, EMPRESS
Company: A.H. Heisey & Company
Years: 1931 – 1938
Colors: crystal, yellow, green,
        pink, alexandrite
Items: 68

PATTERN NAME: FORTUNE
Company: Hocking Glass Company
Years: 1937 – 1938
Colors: pink, crystal
Items: 12

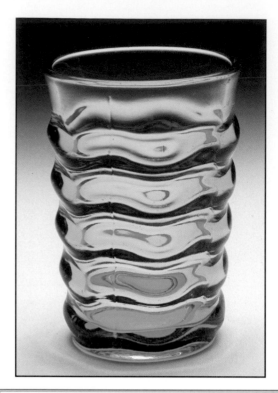

PATTERN NAME: FOUNTAIN, LINE #190
Company: D.C. Jenkins Glass Company
Years: 1920s – 1930s
Colors: green
Items: 23

PATTERN NAME: FRUIT DESIGN,
                            #1058/DELLA ROBIA
Company: Westmoreland Glass Company
Years: 1926 – 1940s; 1950s
Colors: crystal, opal, milk glass,
                   amber, blue, green, pink;
                   stained
Items: 56

PATTERN NAME: FRUITS
Company: Federal Glass Company
Years: 1931 – 1935
Colors: crystal, green, amber, iridescent
Items: 1

PATTERN NAME: FUCHSIA
Company: Tiffin Glass Company
Years: 1937 – 1941
Colors: crystal
Items: 100+

PATTERN NAME: FUCHSIA,
               ETCH #310
Company: Fostoria Glass Company
Years: 1931 – 1944
Colors: crystal, crystal with
            wisteria
Items: 41

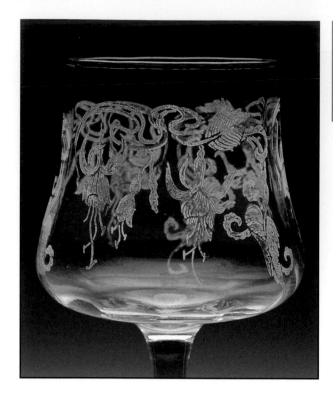

PATTERN NAME: FUCHSIA, #7664 OR MARJORIE
Company: The Cambridge Glass Company
Years: 1915 – 1930s
Colors: crystal
Items: 30+

PATTERN NAME: GADROON, #3500
Company: The Cambridge Glass Company
Years: 1933 – 1958
Colors: crystal, amber, amethyst, red, green, blue, gold decorations
Items: 60+

PATTERN NAME: GAME BIRD
Company: Anchor Hocking Glass Company
Years: 1959 – 1962
Colors: white with decals
Items: 14

PATTERN NAME: GARLAND, #301 LINE
Company: Indiana Glass Company
Years: 1935 – 1950s
Colors: crystal with painted decorations,
          milk glass
Items: 10+

PATTERN NAME: GAZEBO (UTOPIA)
Company: Paden City Glass
         Manufacturing Company
Years: 1930s
Colors: crystal, blue, yellow, black
Items: 21+

PATTERN NAME: GEORGIAN
Company: Federal Glass Company
Years: 1931 – 1936
Colors: green, crystal, amber
Items: 26

PATTERN NAME: GEORGIAN
Company: Hocking Glass Company
Years: 1920s – 1930s
Colors: green, crystal
Items: 9

PATTERN NAME: GLORIA, #746
Company: The Cambridge Glass Company
Years: 1930 – 1934
Colors: crystal; yellow; emerald; amber;
            blue; heatherbloom; peach-blo;
            crystal, cobalt blue, and Crown
            Tuscan with gold decoration;
            black with platinum decoration
Items: 135+

PATTERN NAME: GOLDEN GLORY
Company: Federal Glass Company
Years: 1959 – 1979
Colors: white with gold
Items: 16

PATTERN NAME: GOLDEN SHELL
Company: Anchor Hocking
Glass Company
Years: 1965 – 1976
Colors: white with gold
Items: 14

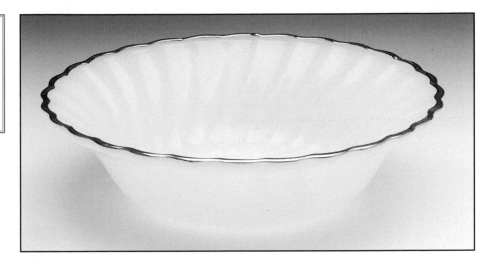

PATTERN NAME: GOLF BALL, #7643 LINE
Company: Morgantown Glass Works
Years: 1932 – 1934
Colors: crystal, red, 3 blues, 3 greens,
yellow, pink, amethyst, teal,
brown, smoke, gold
Items: 26+

PATTERN NAME: GOTHIC GARDEN ETCH
Company: Paden City Glass
Manufacturing Company
Years: 1930s
Colors: yellow, cobalt, pink, crystal,
green, black
Items: 8+

PATTERN NAME: GRAPE BROCADE, #287
Company: Fostoria Glass Company
Years: 1927 – 1930
Colors: blue, green, orchid
Items: 31

PATTERN NAME: GRAPE, CUT 236
Company: Standard Glass
Manufacturing Company
Years: 1930s
Colors: green, yellow, crystal,
pink
Items: 8+

PATTERN NAME: "GRAPE," VINTAGE #14180
Company: Tiffin Glass Company
Years: 1925 – 1932
Colors: crystal, green
Items: 18

PATTERN NAME: GREEK KEY
Company: A.H. Heisey & Company
Years: c. 1912 – 1920s
Colors: crystal, pink
Items: 130+

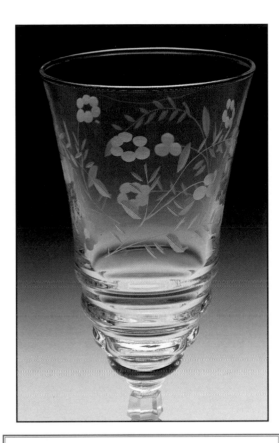

PATTERN NAME: HALIFAX, STEM 3005
Company: Libbey Glass Company
Years: 1940s
Colors: crystal with various cuttings
Items: 20+

PATTERN NAME: HARDING
Company: Central Glass Company
Years: late 1920s – 1930s
Colors: crystal, black, lilac,
          pink, blue
Items: 5+

PATTERN NAME: HARP
Company: Jeannette Glass Company
Years: 1954 – 1957
Colors: crystal, pink, iridescent, white, red, blue, shell pink
Items: 8

PATTERN NAME: HARVEST
Company: Anchor Hocking Glass Company
Years: 1968 – 1971
Colors: white with silver decal
Items: 11

PATTERN NAME: HEATHER, ETCH 343
Company: Fostoria Glass Company
Years: 1949 – 1976
Colors: crystal
Items: 97

PATTERN NAME: HERITAGE
Company: Indiana Glass
　　　　　 Company
Years: 1940 – 1955
Colors: crystal, pink,
　　　　　 blue, green,
　　　　　 cobalt
Items: 10

PATTERN NAME: HERMITAGE, #2449
Company: Fostoria Glass Company
Years: 1932 – 1945
Colors: amber, azure, crystal, black,
　　　　　 green, yellow, wisteria
Items: 59

PATTERN NAME: HEX OPTIC
Company: Jeannette Glass
　　　　　 Company
Years: 1928 – 1932
Colors: pink, green, teal,
　　　　　 iridescent
Items: 30

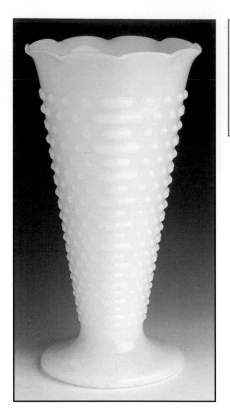

PATTERN NAME: HOBNAIL
Company: Anchor Hocking Glass Company
Years: 1959 – 1979
Colors: milk white; fired-on coral, green, and yellow
Items: 9

PATTERN NAME: HOBNAIL, LINE #118
Company: The Duncan & Miller Glass Company
Years: 1930s – 1940s
Colors: crystal, opalescent yellow, opalescent blue, opalescent pink
Items: 100

PATTERN NAME: HOBNAIL, LINE #118½
Company: The Duncan & Miller Glass Company
Years: 1930s – 1940s
Colors: crystal, opalescent pink, opalescent blue, opalescent yellow
Items: 4

PATTERN NAME: HOBNAIL
Company: Fenton Glass Company
Years: 1950s – 1980s
Colors: milk white
Items: 175+

PATTERN NAME: HOBNAIL
Company: Hocking Glass Company
Years: 1934 – 1936
Colors: crystal, crystal with red, pink
Items: 20

PATTERN NAME: HOLIDAY
Company: Jeannette Glass Company
Years: 1947 – 1950s
Colors: pink, iridescent, shell pink, crystal
Items: 27

PATTERN NAME: HOLLY, CUT 815, #6030 STEMLINE
Company: Fostoria Glass Company
Years: 1942 – 1980
Colors: crystal
Items: 42+

PATTERN NAME: HOMESPUN
Company: Jeannette Glass Company
Years: 1938 – 1940
Colors: pink, crystal
Items: 27

PATTERN NAME: HOMESTEAD
Company: Anchor Hocking Glass Company
Years: 1968 – 1971
Colors: white with decals
Items: 11

PATTERN NAME: HOMESTEAD
Company: L.E. Smith Glass Company
Years: late 1920s
Colors: pink, green, amber, black
Items: 10

PATTERN NAME: HONEYSUCKLE
Company: Anchor Hocking
                 Glass Company
Years: 1959 – 1962
Colors: white with decal
Items: 16

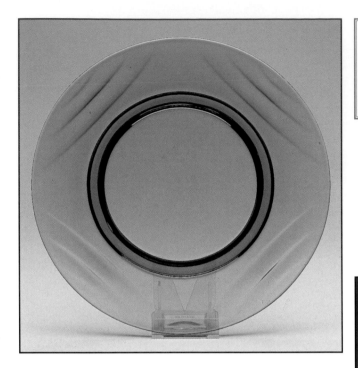

PATTERN NAME: HORIZON, LINES 2650 & 5650
Company: Fostoria Glass Company
Years: 1951 – 1958
Colors: teal (spruce), crystal, cinnamon
Items: 25

PATTERN NAME: "HORSESHOE," #612
Company: Indiana Glass Company
Years: 1930 – 1933
Colors: green, yellow, pink, crystal
Items: 25

PATTERN NAME: HOSTESS LINE
Company: Federal Glass Company
Years: ca. 1930
Colors: green
Items: 3

PATTERN NAME: IMPERIAL HUNT SCENE, #718
Company: The Cambridge Glass Company
Years: 1920s – 1930s
Colors: green; pink; blue; amber; crystal;
             black, emerald, and pink with gold
Items: 50+

PATTERN NAME: INDIANA CUSTARD
Company: Indiana Glass Company
Years: 1930s, 1950s
Colors: ivory, custard, early 1930s;
             white, 1950s; orange blossom
Items: 20

PATTERN NAME: INFORMAL
Company: Hazel-Atlas Glass Company
Years: 1930 – 1935
Colors: platonite with pink, teal,
             black trim
Items: 5

PATTERN NAME: IPSWICH, BLANK 1405
Company: A.H. Heisey & Company, Imperial
Years: 1930s, 1960s
Colors: crystal, pink, yellow, green, cobalt, alexandrite
Items: 23

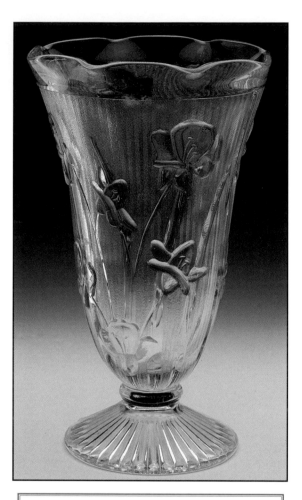

PATTERN NAME: IRIS
Company: Jeannette Glass Company
Years: 1928 – 1970s
Colors: crystal, iridescent, pink, green, white
Items: 40

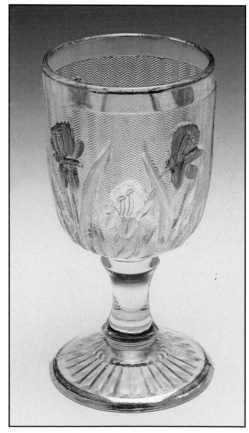

PATTERN NAME: IRIS CORSAGE
Company: Jeannette Glass Company
Years: late 1940s
Colors: crystal with red and gold trim
Items: 5

PATTERN NAME: ISABELLA
Company: Tiffin Glass Company
Years: 1920s – mid-1930s
Colors: crystal
Items: 20+

PATTERN NAME: ITALIAN LACE, #514
Company: Fostoria Glass Company
Years: 1938 – 1944
Colors: crystal with gold
Items: 21

PATTERN NAME: JADE-ITE SHELL
Company: Anchor Hocking Glass Company
Years: 1963 – 1968
Colors: jade-ite
Items: 13

PATTERN NAME: JAMESTOWN, #2719
Company: Fostoria Glass Company
Years: 1958 – 1982
Colors: amber, amethyst, blue, brown, crystal, green, pink, red
Items: 29

PATTERN NAME: JANE RAY
Company: Anchor Hocking Glass Company
Years: 1945 – 1963
Colors: ivory, jade-ite, crystal, white, white with gold, peach lustre, amber
Items: 16

PATTERN NAME: JANICE, LINE #4500
Company: New Martinsville Glass Manufacturing Company, Viking Glass Company
Years: 1940s (New Martinsville) 1945 – 1986 (Viking)
Colors: crystal, cobalt, red, blue, emerald, amethyst
Items: 75+

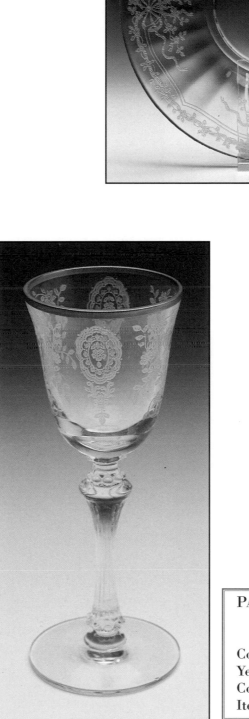

PATTERN NAME: JUBILEE
Company: The Lancaster
           Glass Company
Years: 1930s
Colors: yellow, crystal, pink
Items: 30+

PATTERN NAME: JUNE
Company: Fostoria Glass
           Company
Years: 1928 – 1944
Colors: crystal, blue,
           yellow, pink
Items: 90

PATTERN NAME: JUNE NIGHT/
               CHERRY LAUREL
               (WITH GOLD)
Company: Tiffin Glass Company
Years: 1940s – 1950s
Colors: crystal
Items: 36+

PATTERN NAME: JUNGLE ASSORTMENT, #6207
Company: U.S. Glass Company
Years: 1920s
Colors: satin green, blue, orange
Items: 20+

PATTERN NAME: KASHMIR ETCH #283
Company: Fostoria Glass Company
Years: 1930 – 1934
Colors: green, blue, and yellow
               stems with crystal
Items: 61

PATTERN NAME: KING'S CROWN, 4016 THUMBPRINT
Company: Tiffin Glass Company,
               Indiana Glass Company
Years: 1890s – 1950s (Tiffin)
               1950s – 1980s (Indiana)
Colors: crystal; crystal with ruby, gold, blue, and
               pink; avocado; amber; cobalt
Items: 60+

PATTERN NAME: LA FLEURE
Company: Tiffin Glass Company
Years: 1930s
Colors: yellow, crystal with yellow
Items: 65+

PATTERN NAME: LA FURISTE DESIGN #0907
Company: Lotus Glass Company
Years: 1930s
Colors: crystal, green, pink, amber
Items: 46+

PATTERN NAME: LA FONTAINE, #15033
Company: Tiffin Glass Company
Years: 1924 – 1931
Colors: crystal with green; pink; twilight;
            crystal with gold, pink, or twilight
Items: 14+

PATTERN NAME: LACED EDGE ITAGLIA #7499
Company: Imperial Glass Company
Years: 1930s
Colors: crystal
Items: 10

PATTERN NAME: LAKE COMO
Company: Hocking Glass Company
Years: 1934 – 1937
Colors: white with blue
Items: 13

PATTERN NAME: LARGO
Company: Paden City Glass
          Manufacturing Company
Years: ca. 1930s
Colors: red, blue, crystal
Items: 10+

PATTERN NAME: LARIAT, #1540
Company: A.H. Heisey & Company
Years: ca. 1948
Colors: crystal, amber, black
Items: 78+

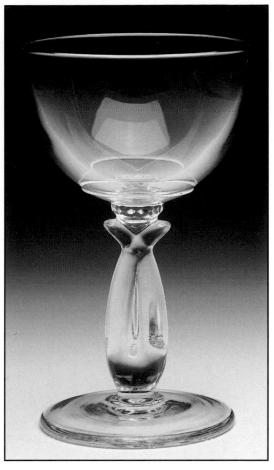

PATTERN NAME: LATTICE DECORATION #314
Company: Westmoreland Glass Company
Years: 1922 – 1930s
Colors: crystal with fired-on black and gray,
                 yellow, opal, green, orange, blue
Items: 10+

PATTERN NAME: LAUREL
Company: Anchor Hocking Glass Company
Years: 1951 – 1965
Colors: gray, peach lustre, jade-ite,
                 ivory, ivory white
Items: 10

PATTERN NAME: LAUREL
Company: McKee Glass Company
Years: ca. 1935 – 1940
Colors: green, blue, ivory, white
Items: 31

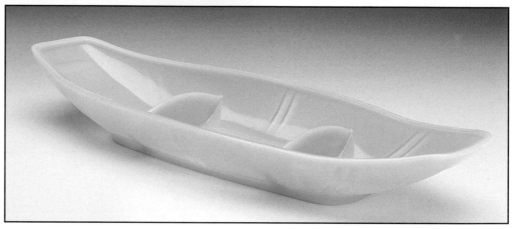

PATTERN NAME: LENOX DESIGN
Company: McKee Glass Company
Years: 1920s – 1930s
Colors: crystal, green, pink, blue, jadite
Items: 42

PATTERN NAME: LIDO, #329
Company: Fostoria Glass Company
Years: 1937 – 1955
Colors: crystal, azure (1938 – 1943)
Items: 70

PATTERN NAME: LILY OF THE VALLEY
Company: The Cambridge Glass Company
Years: ca. 1935
Colors: crystal with frost
Items: 20+

PATTERN NAME: LILY PONS #605
Company: Indiana Glass Company
Years: 1930s
Colors: green
Items: 9

PATTERN NAME: LINCOLN INN, #1700
Company: Fenton Art Glass Company
Years: 1928 – 1940
Colors: crystal, amber, black, emerald,
         pink, cobalt, red, jade, blue
Items: 43+

PATTERN NAME: LINCOLN INN ITAGLIO
#1700 (COLONIAL)
Company: Fenton Art Glass Company
Years: 1940
Colors: crystal
Items: 15

PATTERN NAME: LINE #190-0
Company: New Martinsville Glass
Manufacturing Company
Years: 1920s
Colors: crystal
Items: 1

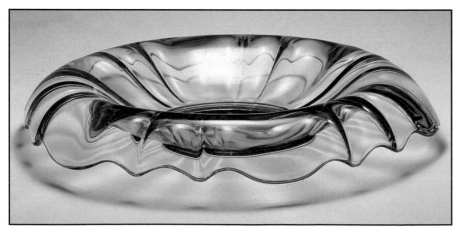

PATTERN NAME: LINE #310
Company: Tiffin Glass Company
Years: late 1920s – 1930s
Colors: pink, green, twilight,
black, old gold
Items: 20+

PATTERN NAME: LINE #351
Company: Standard Glass Company
Years: 1930s
Colors: pink, yellow
Items: 2

PATTERN NAME: LINE #444
Company: Westmoreland Glass Company
Years: 1917 – 1927
Colors: crystal
Items: 15

PATTERN NAME: LINE #520 "BYZANTINE"
Company: The Cambridge Glass Company
Years: 1920s – 1930s
Colors: pink, green
Items: 23+

PATTERN NAME: LINE #555
Company: Canton Glass Company
Years: 1950s
Colors: crystal
Items: 6

PATTERN NAME: LINE #643
Company: Fenton Art Glass Company
Years: ca. 1924
Colors: pekin blue, various blue,
            red, orange
Items: 6

PATTERN NAME: LINE #707 (PEBBLE RIM)
Company: L.E. Smith Glass Company
Years: 1930s
Colors: green, pink, amber, black
Items: 14

PATTERN NAME: LINE #836
Company: Canton Glass Company
Years: 1950s
Colors: crystal, green, cobalt, blue,
amber, red, black, white,
pink
Items: 14

PATTERN NAME: LINE #865
Company: The Lancaster Glass Company
Years: ca. 1932
Colors: pink
Items: 3

PATTERN NAME: LINE #1048
Company: New Martinsville Glass
        Manufacturing
        Company,
        Viking Glass Company
Years: 1920s – 1930s
Colors: crystal
Items: 1

PATTERN NAME: LINE #2425
Company: Fostoria Glass Company
Years: 1930s
Colors: crystal, yellow
Items: 2

PATTERN NAME: LINE #3350S, CUT #2
Company: Standard Glass Company
Years: 1930s
Colors: crystal
Items: 6+

PATTERN NAME: LINE #3400
Company: The Cambridge Glass Company
Years: 1930 – 1940s
Colors: amber, crystal, emerald, blue, crystal
with black, pink, red, heatherbloom
Items: 70+

PATTERN NAME: LINE #4020
Company: Fostoria Glass Company
Years: 1929 – 1934
Colors: crystal; crystal with green,
black, amber, pink, yellow,
or wisteria
Items: 8

PATTERN NAME: "LITTLE (OR NEW)
                 JEWEL," LINE #330,
                 "DIAMOND BLOCK"
Company: Imperial Glass Company
Years: 1930s
Colors: crystal, green, pink, yellow,
          black, carnival
Items: 12

PATTERN NAME: LODESTAR, #1632
Company: A.H. Heisey & Company
Years: ca. 1954
Colors: dawn
Items: 32

PATTERN NAME: LORAIN, #615
Company: Indiana Glass Company
Years: 1929 – 1932
Colors: green, yellow, crystal
Items: 17

PATTERN NAME: LORNA, #748
Company: The Cambridge Glass Company
Years: 1930
Colors: pink, green, crystal
Items: 40+

PATTERN NAME: LOTUS #232
Company: Fostoria Glass Company
Years: 1913 – 1928
Colors: crystal
Items: 110

PATTERN NAME: LOTUS?
Company: Tiffin Glass Company
Years: 1925 – 1932
Colors: crystal with green, black
Items: 15

PATTERN NAME: LOTUS
Company: Westmoreland Glass Company
Years: 1921 – 1970s
Colors: pink, green, crystal, amber,
                various satinized applied colors
Items: 36

PATTERN NAME: LOVEBIRDS WITH GRAPES
Company: Federal Glass Company
Years: 1920s
Colors: crystal with green decorations
Items: 4

PATTERN NAME: LUCIANA
Company: Tiffin Glass Company
Years: 1925 – 1931
Colors: crystal with black, green, or amber
Items: 23

PATTERN NAME: LUCY, PATTERN #895 (BLANK, NOT
SILVER DECORATION) ETCH UNKNOWN
Company: Paden City Glass Manufacturing Company
Years: ca. 1935
Colors: crystal, pink, red, crystal with silver overlay
Items: 5+

PATTERN NAME: MADRID
Company: Federal Glass Company,
Indiana Glass Company
Years: 1932 – 1939 (Federal)
1976 – 1990 (Indiana)
Colors: green, pink, amber,
crystal, blue
Items: 45

PATTERN NAME: MANHATTAN
Company: Anchor Hocking Glass Company
Years: 1938 – 1943
Colors: crystal, pink, green, red, iridescent
Items: 32

PATTERN NAME: MANOR, ETCH #286
Company: Fostoria Glass Company
Years: 1931 – 1944
Colors: green; crystal; yellow;
crystal with green, yellow,
or wisteria
Items: 88

PATTERN NAME: MARTHA WASHINGTON
Company: The Cambridge Glass Company
Years: 1927 – 1940s
Colors: amber, red, crystal, emerald,
blue, green, heatherbloom
Items: 90+

PATTERN NAME: MAYFAIR
Company: Federal Glass Company
Years: 1934
Colors: crystal, amber, green
Items: 13

PATTERN NAME: MAYFAIR
Company: Hocking Glass Company
Years: 1931 – 1937
Colors: crystal, pink, blue, yellow,
green; satinized pink or blue
Items: 63+

PATTERN NAME: MAYFLOWER, #332
Company: Fostoria Glass Company
Years: 1938 – 1955
Colors: crystal
Items: 80+

PATTERN NAME: MEADOW GREEN
Company: Anchor Hocking Glass Company
Years: 1967 – 1977
Colors: white with green decal
Items: 27

PATTERN NAME: MEADOW ROSE
Company: Fostoria Glass Company
Years: 1937 – 1982
Colors: crystal, azure
Items: 68

PATTERN NAME: MEADOW WREATH,
ETCH #26, RADIANCE BLANK
Company: New Martinsville Glass
Manufacturing Company,
Viking Glass Company
Years: 1936 – 1940s (New Martinsville)
after 1944 (Viking)
Colors: crystal
Items: 31

PATTERN NAME: MIDNIGHT ROSE, #316
Company: Fostoria Glass Company
Years: 1933 – 1957
Colors: crystal
Items: 64

PATTERN NAME: MINUET, ETCH #1530
Company: A.H. Heisey & Company
Years: 1939 – 1950s
Colors: crystal
Items: 77

PATTERN NAME: MISS AMERICA
Company: Hocking Glass Company
Years: 1935 – 1938
Colors: crystal, pink, green, blue,
            jade-ite, red
Items: 36

PATTERN NAME: MODERNISTIC, #700
Company: Westmoreland Glass Company
Years: 1927
Colors: crystal, green, yellow
Items: 29

PATTERN NAME: MODERNTONE
Company: Hazel-Atlas Glass Company
Years: 1934 – 1950s
Colors: amethyst, cobalt, crystal,
platonite, pink
Items: 28

PATTERN NAME: "MOLLY," OCTAGON #725
Company: Imperial Glass Company
Years: mid-1930s
Colors: red, blue, pink, green, crystal
Items: 10+

PATTERN NAME: "MOON AND STAR," PALACE
Company: Adam & Company, Fenton Glass Company, L.E. Smith Glass Company, L.G. Wright Glass Company, LeVay Distributing
Years: 1880s; mid-1930s, 1940s – 1980s; 1970s; mid-1970s
Colors: crystal, blue, red, vaseline, green, milk, amethyst, opalescents
Items: 66+

PATTERN NAME: MOONDROPS
Company: New Martinsville Glass Manufacturing Company
Years: 1932 – 1940
Colors: amber, pink, green, cobalt, red, blue, amethyst, crystal, emerald
Items: 78+

PATTERN NAME: MOONSTONE
Company: Anchor Hocking Glass Company
Years: 1941 – 1946
Colors: crystal with opalescent hobs; also pink, green, yellow with opalescence
Items: 22+

PATTERN NAME: MORGAN
Company: Central Glass Company
Years: 1920s – 1930s
Colors: amethyst, black, blue, crystal, green, pink, lilac
Items: 43+

PATTERN NAME: MORNING GLORY,
CARVING #12
Company: Fostoria Glass Company
Years: 1939 – 1944
Colors: crystal, light blue
Items: 44

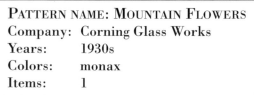

PATTERN NAME: MOROCCAN AMETHYST
Company: Hazel Ware Glass Company
Years: 1960s
Colors: amethyst
Items: 36+

PATTERN NAME: MOUNTAIN FLOWERS
Company: Corning Glass Works
Years: 1930s
Colors: monax
Items: 1

PATTERN NAME: MT. PLEASANT
Company: L.E. Smith Glass
            Company
Years: 1920s – 1934
Colors: black, amethyst,
            cobalt, crystal,
            pink, green, white
Items: 36+

PATTERN NAME: MT. VERNON
Company: The Cambridge Glass
            Company
Years: 1920s – 1940s
Colors: amber, crystal, red, cobalt,
            emerald, heatherbloom
Items: 126+

PATTERN NAME: MT. VERNON
Company: Imperial Glass
            Company
Years: 1930s
Colors: crystal
Items: 35

PATTERN NAME: NARROW FLUTE, #393
Company: A.H. Heisey & Company
Years: ca. 1911
Colors: crystal
Items: 153+

PATTERN NAME: NATIONAL
Company: Jeannette Glass Company
Years: later 1940s – 1950s
Colors: crystal, pink, shell pink, red
and blue flashed
Items: 25+

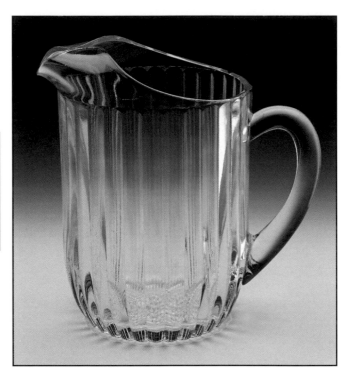

PATTERN NAME: NAVARRE, ETCH #327
Company: Fostoria Glass Company,
Lenox Glass Company
Years: 1937 – 1982 (Fostoria)
after 1982 (Lenox)
Colors: crystal, azure and pink with
crystal
Items: 150+

PATTERN NAME: NEW CENTURY
Company: Hazel-Atlas Glass Company
Years: 1930 – 1935
Colors: crystal, pink, amethyst,
                 green, cobalt
Items: 32

PATTERN NAME: NEW ERA #4044
Company: A.H. Heisey & Company
Years: 1935 – 1957
Colors: crystal, cobalt, crystal
                 with satin
Items: 30+

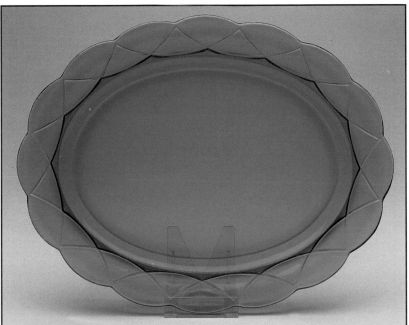

PATTERN NAME: NEWPORT
Company: Hazel-Atlas Glass Company
Years: 1936 – 1940
Colors: cobalt, amethyst, pink,
                 white, white with fired-on
                 color
Items: 16

PATTERN NAME: NEW VINTAGE,
            ETCH #227
Company: Fostoria Glass Company
Years: 1913 – 1928
Colors: crystal
Items: 180

PATTERN NAME: NORMANDIE
Company: Federal Glass Company
Years: 1933 – 1940
Colors: amber, pink, crystal, iridescent
Items: 21

PATTERN NAME: OCTAGON,
            #1231
Company: A.H. Heisey &
          Company
Years: 1926
Colors: crystal, pink, yellow,
          green, orchid,
          marigold, dawn
Items: 41+

PATTERN NAME: OCTAVE
Company: Morgantown Glass Works
Years: ca. 1935
Colors: crystal with red, blue, or green
Items: 5

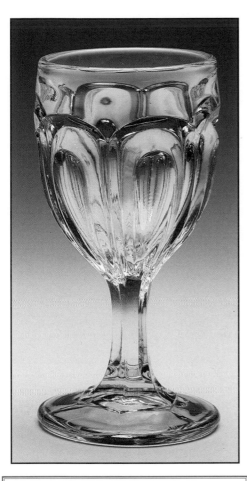

PATTERN NAME: O'HARA
Company: McKee Glass Company
Years: 1890s
Colors: crystal
Items: 3+

PATTERN NAME: OLD CAFE
Company: Hocking Glass Company
Years: 1936 – 1940
Colors: pink, crystal, red
Items: 19

PATTERN NAME: OLD COLONY, #1401,
3390, 3380
Company: A.H. Heisey & Company
Years: 1930 – 1939
Colors: crystal, pink, yellow, green,
marigold
Items: 95+

PATTERN NAME: OLD ENGLISH
THREADING
Company: Indiana Glass Company
Years: later 1930s
Colors: green, amber, pink, crystal,
crystal with fired-on colors,
emerald
Items: 26

PATTERN NAME: OLD COLONY,
"LACE EDGE"
Company: Hocking Glass Company
Years: 1935 – 1938
Colors: pink, crystal, satinized
Items: 36

PATTERN NAME: OLD SANDWICH, #1404
Company: A. H. Heisey & Company
Years: 1926
Colors: crystal, pink, yellow, green, cobalt, amber
Items: 47

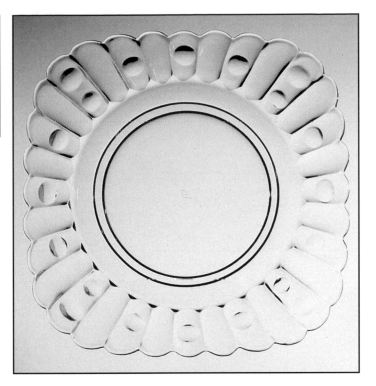

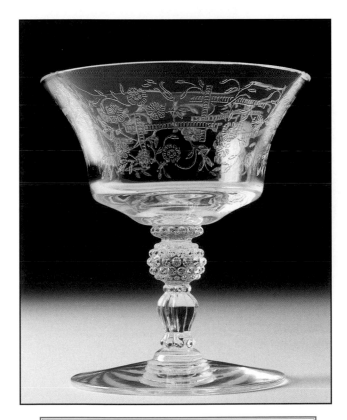

PATTERN NAME: OLYMPIAD ETCH
(TRELLIS ROSE) #458
Company: A.H. Heisey & Company
Years: 1933 – 1942
Colors: crystal, yellow
Items: 130+

PATTERN NAME: OPAL LINE #9
Company: McKee/Thatcher Glass Company
Years: 1950 – 1952
Colors: crystal, milk glass
Items: 5

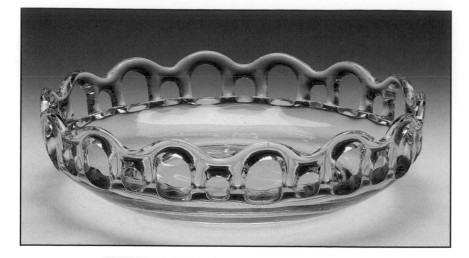

PATTERN NAME: OPEN WORK, #906
Company: Lancaster Glass Company
Years: 1930s
Colors: pink, yellow
Items: 24

PATTERN NAME: ORCHID
Company: Paden City Glass
          Manufacturing
          Company
Years: 1930s
Colors: yellow, cobalt,
          crystal, green,
          amber, pink,
          red, black
Items: 19+

PATTERN NAME: ORCHID ETCH #1507 – VARIOUS BLANKS
Company: A.H. Heisey & Company
Years: 1940 – 1957
Colors: crystal
Items: 230+

PATTERN NAME: OVIDE
Company: Hazel-Atlas Glass Company
Years: 1930 – 1935
Colors: black, green, white with colors
Items: 16

PATTERN NAME: OYSTER & PEARL
Company: Anchor Hocking Glass
Company
Years: 1938 – 1940
Colors: pink; crystal; red;
vitrock; vitrock with
pink, blue, or green
Items: 7

PATTERN NAME: PANELED GRAPE, #1881
Company: Westmoreland Glass Company
Years: 1950s – 1970s
Colors: white, white with decals, green
Items: 158+

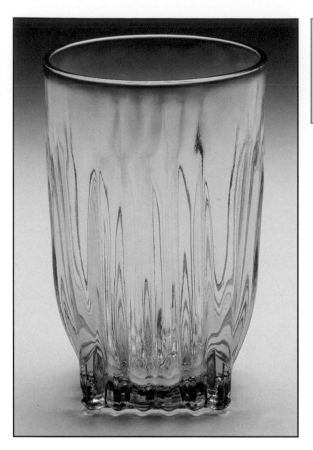

PATTERN NAME: PARK AVE
Company: Federal Glass Company
Years: 1941 – 1970
Colors: crystal, amber
Items: 10

PATTERN NAME: PARK LANE
Company: Colony Glass Company
Years: 1950s – 1960s
Colors: crystal, smoky green,
            smoky blue, smoke, amber
Items: 4+

PATTERN NAME: "PARROT"/SYLVAN
Company: Federal Glass Company
Years: 1931 – 1932
Colors: green, amber, crystal, blue
Items: 25

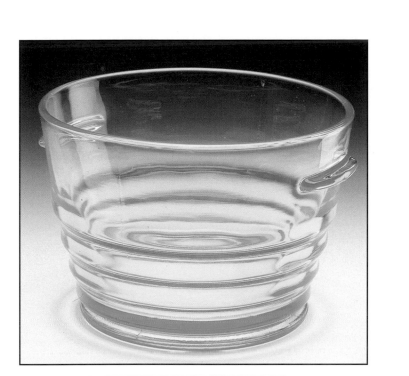

PATTERN NAME: PARTY LINE #191
AND 191½
Company: Paden City Glass
Manufacturing Company
Years: 1920s – 1950s
Colors: green, pink, amber, blue,
red
Items: 56+

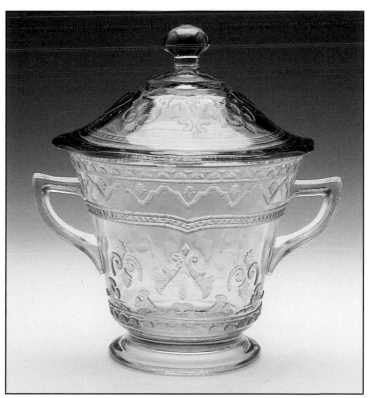

PATTERN NAME: PATRICIAN
Company: Federal Glass Company
Years: 1933 – 1937
Colors: pink, green, crystal, amber
Items: 29

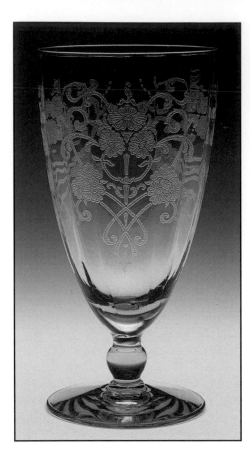

PATTERN NAME: PATRICK
Company: Lancaster Glass Company
Years: 1930s
Colors: yellow, pink
Items: 19

PATTERN NAME: PATTERN #348
Company: Tiffin Glass Company
Years: 1926 – 1933
Colors: crystal, pink, green, amber
Items: 15

PATTERN NAME: PATTERN #500
Company: Jeannette Glass Company
Years: ca. 1939
Colors: pink (wild rose)
Items: 3

PATTERN NAME: PEACH LUSTRE SHELL
Company: Anchor Hocking Glass Company
Years: 1965 – 1976
Colors: lustre
Items: 15

PATTERN NAME: PEACOCK & WILD ROSE (NORA BIRD)
Company: Paden City Glass Manufacturing Company
Years: 1930s
Colors: pink, green, amber, cobalt, black, blue, crystal, red
Items: 40+

PATTERN NAME: PEACOCK ETCH #366,
                STEM 3308
Company: A.H. Heisey & Company
Years: 1916 – 1928
Colors: crystal
Items: 49+

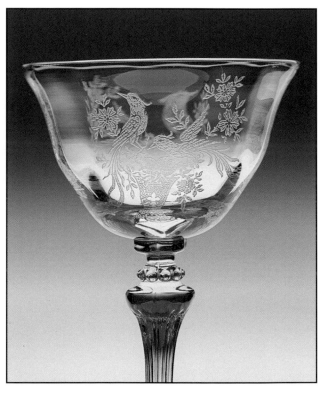

PATTERN NAME: PERSIAN PHEASANT
Company: Tiffin Glass Company
Years: 1930 – 1935
Colors: crystal, pink, crystal with
        green
Items: 30+

PATTERN NAME: "PEACOCK
               REVERSE"
Company: Paden City Glass
         Manufacturing Company
Years: 1930s
Colors: cobalt, red, amber,
        yellow, green, pink,
        black, crystal
Items: 20+

PATTERN NAME: PETAL #2829
Company: Federal Glass Company
Years: 1950s – 1970s
Colors: crystal, yellow, flashed colors
Items: 6+

PATTERN NAME: PETAL FOOT STEM
Company: Weston Glass Company, Fry Glass Company (larger petals)
Years: 1930s
Colors: crystal with black, cobalt, red
Items: 6+

PATTERN NAME: PETALWARE
Company: MacBeth-Evans Glass Company
Years: 1930s – 1940s
Colors: monax, cremax, pink, crystal, cobalt, colors fired-on crystal
Items: 24

PATTERN NAME: "PHILBE"
Company: Anchor Hocking Glass Company
Years: 1937 – 1938
Colors: blue, green, pink, crystal
Items: 21+

PATTERN NAME: PIED PIPER #439
Company: A.H. Heisey & Company
Years: ca. 1924 – 1942
Colors: crystal
Items: 31

PATTERN NAME: PILAR OPTIC
Company: Anchor Hocking
        Glass Company
Years: 1937 – 1942
Colors: crystal, green,
        pink, red
Items: 15+

PATTERN NAME: PINEAPPLE & FLORAL, #618
Company: Indiana Glass Company
Years: 1932 – 1980s
Colors: crystal, amber, green, pink, fired red, avocado, cobalt
Items: 23

PATTERN NAME: PIONEER
Company: Federal Glass Company
Years: 1930s – 1970s
Colors: crystal, pink, smoke, goofus
Items: 12

PATTERN NAME: PIONEER #2350
Company: Fostoria Glass Company
Years: 1925 – 1941
Colors: amber, blue, green, crystal
Items: 50+

PATTERN NAME: PLANTATION, #1567 & 5067
Company: A.H. Heisey & Company
Years: 1949 – 1957
Colors: crystal, amber
Items: 74

PATTERN NAME: PLEAT & PANEL, #1770
Company: A.H. Heisey & Company
Years: 1924 – 1930s
Colors: crystal, pink, green
Items: 33

PATTERN NAME: PLUME, CUT #839
Company: Fostoria Glass Company
Years: 1954 – 1960
Colors: crystal
Items: 26

PATTERN NAME: PLYMOUTH, #1620
Company: Fenton Glass Company
Years: 1930s
Colors: amber, crystal, opalescent, blue, red, green
Items: 20

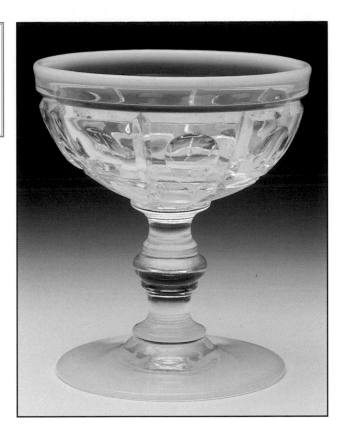

PATTERN NAME: PORTIA, ETCH #754
Company: The Cambridge Glass Company
Years: 1932 – 1940s
Colors: crystal; crystal, black, and Crown Tuscan with gold; yellow; green; heatherbloom; carmen with gold
Items: 125+

PATTERN NAME: PRELUDE
Company: New Martinsville Glass Manufacturing Company, Viking Glass Company
Years: 1930s – 1950s
Colors: crystal
Items: 100+

PATTERN NAME: PRETZEL, #622
Company: Indiana Glass Company
Years: 1930s – 1980s
Colors: crystal, teal, avocado,
          amber, blue
Items: 21

PATTERN NAME: PRIMO
Company: U.S. Glass Company
Years: 1930s
Colors: green, yellow
Items: 16

PATTERN NAME: PRIMROSE
Company: Anchor Hocking Glass Company
Years: 1960 – 1962
Colors: white with pink flower decal
Items: 38

PATTERN NAME: PRINCESS
Company: Hocking Glass Company
Years: 1931 – 1935
Colors: green, yellow, apricot, pink,
            blue, satinized pink or green
Items: 40+

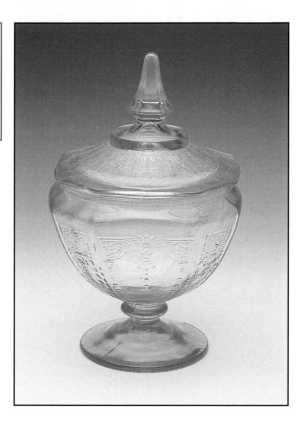

PATTERN NAME: PRINCESS, #643
Company: Tiffin Glass Company
Years: 1920s
Colors: crystal
Items: 30

PATTERN NAME: PRISCILLA, #2321
Company: Fostoria Glass Company
Years: 1925 – 1930
Colors: green, amber, blue, pink, azure
Items: 9

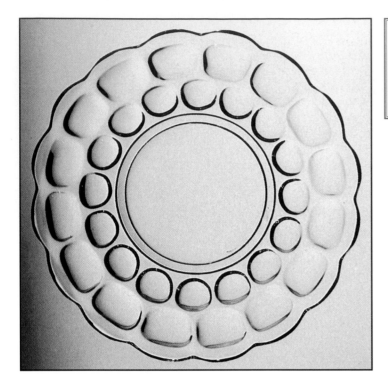

PATTERN NAME: PROVINCIAL, BLANK #1506
Company: A.H. Heisey & Company
Years: 1938 – 1950s
Colors: crystal, zircon
Items: 48

PATTERN NAME: PSYCHE, #14194
Company: Tiffin Glass Company
Years: 1926 – 1931
Colors: crystal with green
Items: 22+

PATTERN NAME: "PYRAMID,"
#610
Company: Indiana Glass
Company
Years: 1926 – 1932;
1974 – 1975
Colors: green, pink,
yellow, white,
crystal; blue,
black
Items: 13

PATTERN NAME: QUADRANGLE, #2546
Company: Fostoria Glass Company
Years: late 1930s
Colors: blue, yellow, crystal
Items: 3

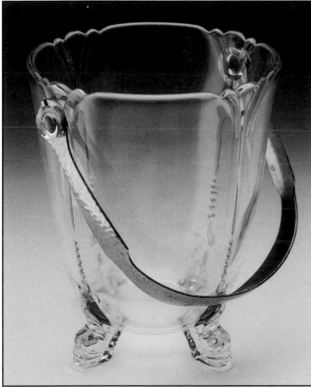

PATTERN NAME: QUEEN ANN, BLANK #1401
Company: A.H. Heisey & Company
Years: 1938 – 1950s
Colors: crystal
Items: 90

PATTERN NAME: QUEEN ANNE, ETCH 306
Company: Fostoria Glass Company
Years: 1929 – 1934
Colors: crystal, amber with crystal
Items: 42

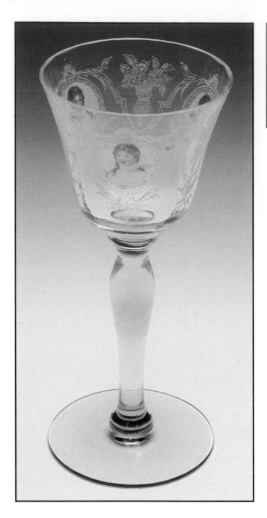

PATTERN NAME: QUEEN LOUISE, #7614 HAMPTON STEM
Company: Morgantown Glass Works
Years: 1928
Colors: silk screen print with pink
Items: 7+

PATTERN NAME: QUEEN MARY
Company: Anchor Hocking Glass Company
Years: 1936 – 1949
Colors: pink, crystal, red
Items: 38

PATTERN NAME: RADIANCE LINE #42
Company: New Martinsville Glass
               Manufacturing Company,
               Viking Glass Company
Years: 1930s – 1940s (New Martinsville)
               after 1944 – 1980s (Viking)
Colors: crystal, amber, cobalt, blue, light
               blue, red, pink, green
Items: 40+

PATTERN NAME: RADIANCE, CUT #409
Company: New Martinsville Glass
           Manufacturing Company
Years: 1930s – 1940s
Colors: crystal
Items: 15

PATTERN NAME: RAINDROPS
Company: Federal Glass Company
Years: 1929 – 1933
Colors: green, crystal
Items: 20

PATTERN NAME: REEDED, #701 (ALSO SPUN)
Company: Imperial Glass Company
Years: 1936
Colors: red, green, crystal, amber, cobalt
Items: 24

PATTERN NAME: REGENCY, CUT #744,
             WESTCHESTER STEM
Company: Fostoria Glass Company
Years: 1935 – 1943
Colors: crystal
Items: 36

PATTERN NAME: REGINA #210 (BLANK)
Company: Paden City Glass
                 Manufacturing Company
Years: 1930s
Colors: pink, green, blue, yellow
Items: 42+

PATTERN NAME: REPEAL, #38
Company: New Martinsville
          Glass Manufacturing
          Company
Years: ca. 1933 – 1935
Colors: crystal, amber, red,
            green, cobalt
Items: 10

PATTERN NAME: RESTAURANT WARE
Company: Anchor Hocking Glass Company
Years: 1948 – 1967
Colors: white, azur-ite, crystal, jade-ite, rose-ite
Items: 29

PATTERN NAME: REVERE, ETCH 1009 (P), DEC. #109 (WITH GOLD)
Company: Lotus Glass Company
Years: 1930s
Colors: pink, crystal with green or pink with gold trim
Items: 28

PATTERN NAME: RHONDO, #7966
Company: The Cambridge Glass Company
Years: 1951 – 1958
Colors: crystal
Items: 30

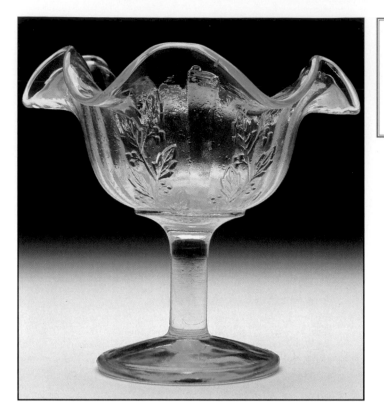

PATTERN NAME: RIB & HOLLY SPRIG
Company: Fenton Glass Company
Years: ca. 1925 – 1930s
Colors: gold, red, blue, violet, pink, green
Items: 3

PATTERN NAME: RIBBON
Company: Hazel-Atlas Glass Company
Years: 1930s
Colors: green, black, crystal, pink
Items: 13

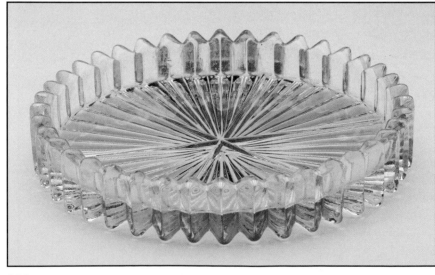

PATTERN NAME: RIDGELEIGH #1469
Company: A.H. Heisey & Company
Years: 1936 – 1940
Colors: crystal, pink, zircon, yellow, dawn
Items: 114

PATTERN NAME: RING
Company: Hocking Glass Company
Years: 1927 – 1933
Colors: crystal, green, pink, blue, red, crystal
            with silver, colored bands, yellow
Items: 37

PATTERN NAME: RINGS OF GOLD, #196
Company: Tiffin Glass Company
Years: 1931 – 1940
Colors: crystal with gold
Items: 30

PATTERN NAME: RIPPLE (ALSO "CRINOLINE")
Company: Hazel-Atlas Glass Company
Years: 1950s
Colors: white, white with pink, white with blue
Items: 13

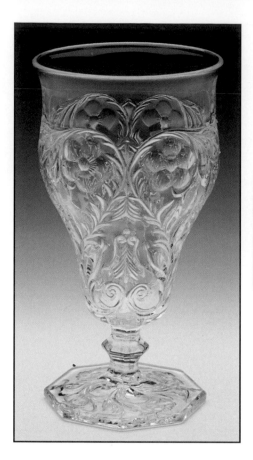

PATTERN NAME: ROCK CRYSTAL
Company: McKee Glass Company
Years: 1920s – 1940s
Colors: crystal, green, yellow, amber, pink, red,
          milk glass, cobalt, blue, satinized colors
Items: 76+

PATTERN NAME: ROCK CRYSTAL
Company: Tiffin Glass Company
Years: 1925 – 1938
Colors: crystal
Items: 14+

PATTERN NAME: ROMANCE, ETCH #341
Company: Fostoria Glass Company
Years: 1942 – 1972
Colors: crystal
Items: 78

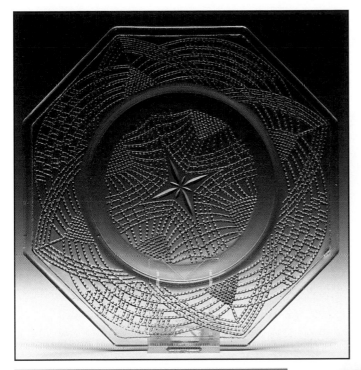

PATTERN NAME: ROMANESQUE
Company: L.E. Smith Glass Company
Years: 1930s
Colors: amber, crystal, yellow,
               green, black, pink
Items: 12+

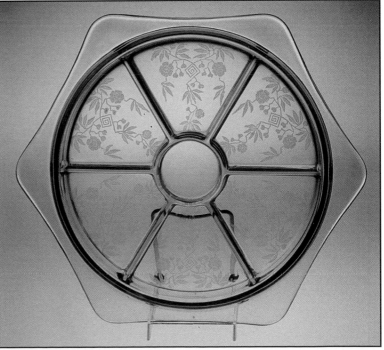

PATTERN NAME: ROSALIE, #731
Company: The Cambridge Glass Company
Years: 1920s – 1930s
Colors: blue, green, heatherbloom, pink,
               red, amber, crystal, yellow
Items: 80+

PATTERN NAME: ROSE AND THORN
Company: U.S. Glass Company
Years: 1930s
Colors: green, pink, black, crystal
Items: 2

PATTERN NAME: ROSE CAMEO
Company: Belmont Tumbler Glass Company
Years: 1931
Colors: green
Items: 6

PATTERN NAME: ROSE, RADIANT ROSE
Company: Cambridge Glass Company
Years: 1957 – 1958
Colors: crystal
Items: 7

PATTERN NAME: ROSE, ETCH #1515
Company: A.H. Heisey & Company
Years: 1949 – 1957
Colors: crystal
Items: 100+

PATTERN NAME: ROSEMARY
Company: Federal Glass Company
Years: 1935 – 1937
Colors: amber, green, pink, iridescent
Items: 13

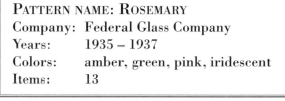

PATTERN NAME: ROSEPOINT
Company: The Cambridge Glass Company
Years: 1936 – 1953
Colors: crystal, Crown Tuscan, black,
            red, blue, amber, all with gold
Items: 403+

PATTERN NAME: ROSE-ITE SWIRL
Company: Anchor Hocking Glass Company
Years: 1950s
Colors: pink opaque
Items: 10

PATTERN NAME: ROULETTE
Company: Hocking Glass Company
Years: 1935 – 1939
Colors: pink, green, crystal
Items: 14

PATTERN NAME: ROUND ROBIN
Company: Unknown
Years: 1930s
Colors: green, iridescent, crystal
Items: 10

PATTERN NAME: ROXANA
Company: Hazel-Atlas Glass Company
Years: 1932
Colors: yellow, crystal, white
Items: 7

PATTERN NAME: ROYAL, ETCH #273
Company: Fostoria Glass Company
Years: 1925 – 1934
Colors: crystal, green, blue, amber
Items: 86

PATTERN NAME: ROYAL LACE
Company: Hazel-Atlas Glass Company
Years: 1934 – 1941
Colors: cobalt, crystal, green, pink,
amethyst
Items: 39

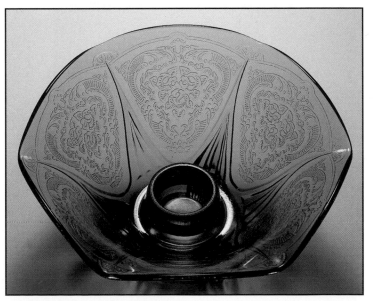

PATTERN NAME: ROYAL RUBY
Company: Anchor Hocking Glass Company
Years: 1937 – 1977
Colors: red
Items: 56+

PATTERN NAME: RUBA ROMBIC
Company: Consolidated Lamp and Glass Company
Years: 1928 – 1933
Colors: smoky topaz, jungle green, French
            crystal, silver gray, lilac, sunshine,
            jade, milk glass, apple green, black,
            French opalescent
Items: 37

PATTERN NAME: S PATTERN
Company: MacBeth-Evans Glass Company
Years: 1930 – 1935
Colors: crystal; crystal with trims of amber,
            green, and blue; pink; amber;
            green; red; monax; yellow
Items: 19

PATTERN NAME: SANDWICH
Company: Hocking Glass Company
Years: 1939 – 1993
Colors: crystal, amber, forest green, pink, red, milk glass
Items: 40

PATTERN NAME: SANDWICH
Company: Indiana Glass Company
Years: 1920s – 1980s
Colors: crystal, teal, white, amber, red, blue, pink, green
Items: 39+

PATTERN NAME: SANDWICH, EARLY AMERICAN
PATTERN #41
Company: Duncan Glass Company
Years: 1924 – 1955
Colors: crystal, green, red, cobalt, milk glass
Items: 140

PATTERN NAME: SANIBEL #130
Company: Duncan Glass Company
Years: 1940s
Colors: crystal; opalescent blue, pink, or yellow
Items: 28

PATTERN NAME: SATURN, BLANK #1485
Company: A.H. Heisey & Company
Years: 1937 – 1950s
Colors: crystal, zircon, dawn
Items: 55

PATTERN NAME: SCEPTRE STEM #6017
Company: Fostoria Glass Company
Years: 1937 – 1971
Colors: crystal, azure, gold tint
Items: 12

PATTERN NAME: SCROLL FLUTED
Company: Imperial Glass Company
Years: 1930s
Colors: pink, green, crystal
Items: 13

PATTERN NAME: SEASCAPE #2685
Company: Fostoria Glass Company
Years: 1954 – 1958
Colors: opalescent blue, opalescent pink
Items: 19

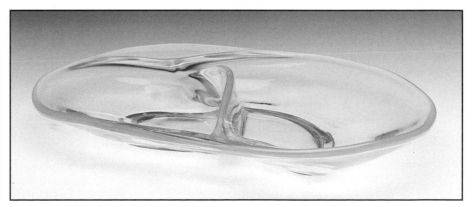

PATTERN NAME: SEVILLE, ETCH #274
Company: Fostoria Glass Company
Years: 1926 – 1934
Colors: crystal, amber, blue, green
Items: 86

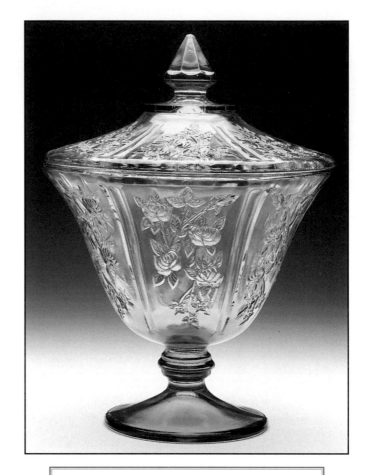

PATTERN NAME: SHARON
Company: Federal Glass Company
Years: 1935 – 1939
Colors: pink, green, crystal, amber
Items: 32

PATTERN NAME: SHEFFIELD, #1800
Company: Fenton Glass Company
Years: 1936 – 1938
Colors: crystal, satin crystal, aqua,
blue, gold, red, amber, wisteria
Items: 30

PATTERN NAME: SHELL PINK
Company: Jeannette Glass Company
Years: 1957 – 1959
Colors: opaque pink
Items: 53+

PATTERN NAME: SHIPS
Company: Hazel-Atlas Glass Company
Years: 1930s
Colors: cobalt with white, red, or yellow, crystal with blue
Items: 21

PATTERN NAME: SHIRLEY (TEMPLE) ETCH #331
Company: Fostoria Glass Company
Years: 1939 – 1957
Colors: crystal
Items: 62

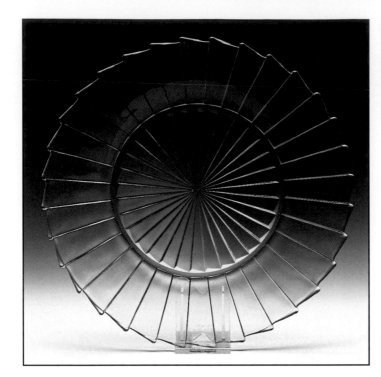

PATTERN NAME: SIERRA
Company: Jeannette Glass Company
Years: 1931 – 1933
Colors: pink, green, teal
Items: 15

PATTERN NAME: SILVER CREST
Company: Fenton Art Glass Company
Years: 1943 – present
Colors: white with crystal edge
Items: 125+

PATTERN NAME: SNOWFLAKE
Company: Jeannette Glass Company
Years: 1930s
Colors: pink, green
Items: 2

PATTERN NAME: SODA FOUNTAIN, #304
Company: Indiana Glass Company
Years: 1930s
Colors: pink, green, crystal
Items: 18

PATTERN NAME: SPARTAN (NEEDLE),
ETCH #80
Company: Fostoria Glass Company
Years: 1927 – 1944
Colors: crystal, amber, orchid
with crystal, green with
crystal
Items: 24

PATTERN NAME: SPHINX
Company: The Lancaster Glass
Company
Years: 1930s
Colors: green, yellow
Items: 3

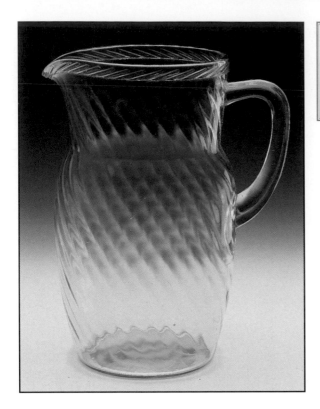

PATTERN NAME: SPIRAL
Company: Hocking Glass Company
Years: 1928 – 1930
Colors: pink, green, crystal
Items: 20

PATTERN NAME: SPIRAL FLUTES #40
Company: Duncan Glass Company
Years: 1924
Colors: amber, green, pink, crystal,
crystal with amber
Items: 72+

PATTERN NAME: SPOKE LINE #15359
Company: Tiffin Glass Company
Years: 1937 – 1941
Colors: pink, green, crystal, yellow
Items: 24

PATTERN NAME: SPOKE OR "WAGON WHEEL"
Company: Unknown
Years: ca. 1930s
Colors: crystal, crystal with trims, pink, green
Items: 5

PATTERN NAME: SPOOL PATTERN #2550
Company: Fostoria Glass Company
Years: 1938 – 1944
Colors: blue, gold tint, crystal
Items: 20

PATTERN NAME: SPRINGTIME
Company: Lotus Glass Company
Years: 1930s
Colors: pink, white with silver, crystal
Items: 45

PATTERN NAME: SPRINGTIME, #270
Company: The Monongah Glass Company
Years: 1920s
Colors: crystal
Items: 21

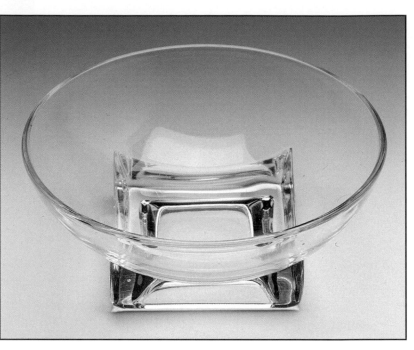

PATTERN NAME: SQUARE
Company: The Cambridge Glass Company
Years: 1952 – 1957
Colors: crystal, red, black
Items: 69+

PATTERN NAME: STANHOPE, #1483
Company: A.H. Heisey & Company
Years: 1936 – 1941
Colors: crystal, zircon
Items: 44

PATTERN NAME: STAR
Company: Federal Glass Company
Years: 1950s
Colors: amber, crystal, crystal with gold
Items: 16

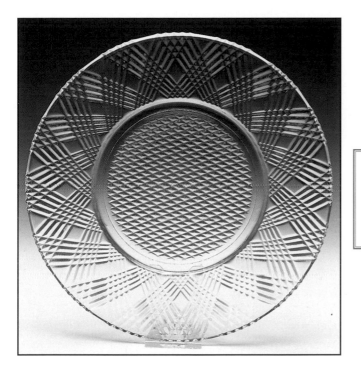

PATTERN NAME: STARLIGHT
Company: Hazel-Atlas Glass Company
Years: 1938 – 1940
Colors: crystal, pink, white, cobalt
Items: 15

PATTERN NAME: STARS & STRIPES
Company: Anchor Hocking Glass Company
Years: 1942
Colors: crystal
Items: 3

PATTERN NAME: STEM 3005, NORMANDIE,
              TROPIC ROSE
Company: Libbey Glass Company
Years: 1940s
Colors: crystal with various cuttings
Items: 20+

PATTERN NAME: STERLING FLORAL
Company: Hazel-Atlas Glass Company
Years: ca. 1930s
Colors: black with sterling
Items: 9

PATTERN NAME: STRAWBERRY
Company: U.S. Glass Company
Years: 1930s
Colors: pink, green, crystal,
              iridescent
Items: 20

PATTERN NAME: STRING OF PEARLS
Company: Westmoreland Glass Company
Years: 1918 – 1933
Colors: blue, yellow, and white; or green, yellow, and white
Items: 7+

PATTERN NAME: SUNBURST
Company: Jeannette Glass Company
Years: later 1930s
Colors: crystal
Items: 15

PATTERN NAME: SUNFLOWER
Company: Jeannette Glass Company
Years: 1930s
Colors: pink, green, delphite, ultra-marine
Items: 10

PATTERN NAME: SUNRAY, LINE #2510
Company: Fostoria Glass Company
Years: 1935 – 1944
Colors: crystal, red, blue, green, yellow
Items: 87

PATTERN NAME: SUNRISE SWIRL
Company: Anchor Hocking Glass Company
Years: 1950s
Colors: ivory with red trim
Items: 13

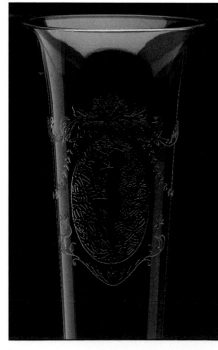

PATTERN NAME: SUNRISE MEDALLION, #758
Company: Morgantown Glass Works
Years: later 1920s – 1930
Colors: pink, green, crystal, blue
Items: 28+

PATTERN NAME: SUNSHINE #734
Company: The Lancaster Glass Company
Years: 1930s
Colors: pink, green, blue
Items: 36

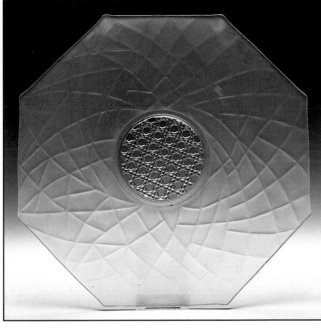

PATTERN NAME: SWAN
Company: The Cambridge Glass
Company
Years: 1930s
Colors: crystal, green, pink,
Crown Tuscan, black,
yellow, white, red,
moonlight blue
Items: 15

PATTERN NAME: SWIRL
Company: Jeannette Glass Company
Years: 1937 – 1938
Colors: teal, pink, delphite,
amber, blue
Items: 35

PATTERN NAME: SWIRL, FIRE-KING
Company: Anchor Hocking Glass Company
Years: 1949 – 1962
Colors: pink, opaque blue, ivory, white, jade-ite, peach lustre, ivory with red, white or ivory with gold
Items: 19+

PATTERN NAME: SYLVAN #122
Company: Duncan Glass Company
Years: c. 1940
Colors: crystal, crystal with trim
Items: 25

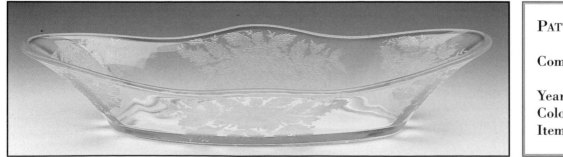

PATTERN NAME: SYLVAN #151
Company: Tiffin Glass Company
Years: 1925 – 1935
Colors: pink, green
Items: 17

PATTERN NAME: TALLY HO LINE #1402
Company: The Cambridge Glass Company
Years: 1932 – 1940s
Colors: amber, amethyst, red, crystal,
            green, blue, gold
Items: 70+

PATTERN NAME: TEA ROOM
Company: Indiana Glass Company
Years: 1926 – 1931
Colors: pink, green, crystal,
            amber
Items: 45

PATTERN NAME: TEARDROP #301
Company: Duncan Glass Company
Years: 1936 – 1955
Colors: crystal
Items: 130+

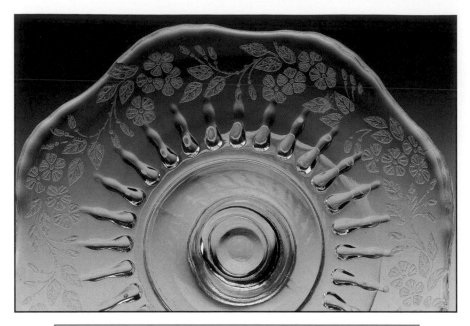

PATTERN NAME: TEARDROP, LINE #4400, ETCH #26
(MEADOW WREATH)
Company: New Martinsville Glass Manufacturing
Company, Viking Glass Company
Years: 1940s, 1980s
Colors: crystal, red, blue, yellow, cobalt
Items: 20

PATTERN NAME: TERRACE, #111
Company: The Duncan & Miller Glass Company
Years: 1937 – 1940s
Colors: crystal, cobalt, red, amber
Items: 75

PATTERN NAME: THISTLE, CAMBRIDGE #1066
Company: The Cambridge Glass Company
Years: late 1940s – 1950s
Colors: crystal
Items: 15+

PATTERN NAME: THISTLE
Company: Fry Glass Company
Years: later 1920s – 1930
Colors: pink, blue
Items: 7

PATTERN NAME: THISTLE
Company: MacBeth-Evans Glass Company
Years: 1929 – 1930
Colors: pink, green, crystal, yellow
Items: 7

PATTERN NAME: THOUSAND EYE
Company: Westmoreland Glass Company
Years: 1934 – 1956
Colors: crystal
Items: 98+

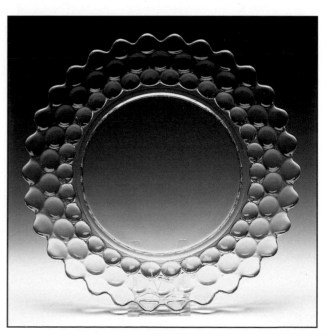

PATTERN NAME: THUMBPRINT
Company: Federal Glass Company
Years: 1930s
Colors: green
Items: 18+

PATTERN NAME: TINKERBELL, ETCH #756,
                        #7631 JEWEL STEM
Company: Morgantown Glass Works
Years: 1927 – 1931
Colors: azure, green
Items: 9

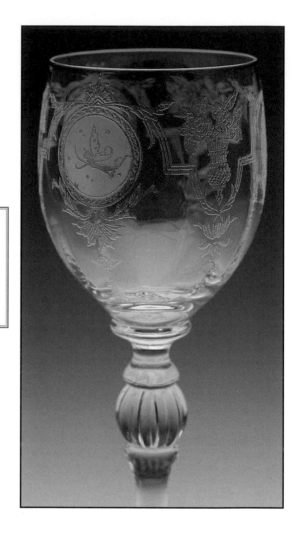

PATTERN NAME: TOURAINNE #17328
                        STEM, #11 ROSE
Company: Tiffin Glass Company
Years: late 1920s – 1930s
Colors: crystal
Items: 15+

PATTERN NAME: TRADITION
Company: Imperial Glass Company
Years: 1950s
Colors: blue, crystal, red, green, pink, amber
Items: 15+

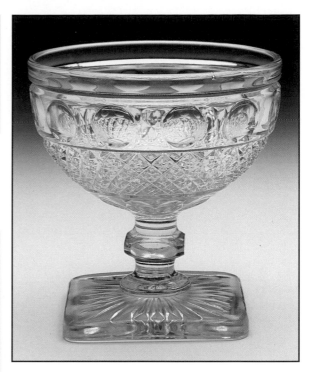

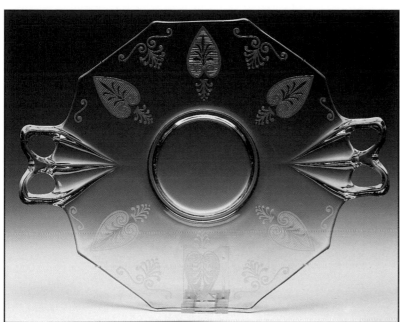

PATTERN NAME: TROJAN ETCH #280
Company: Fostoria Glass Company
Years: 1930s – 1944
Colors: pink, yellow
Items: 100+

PATTERN NAME: TULIP
Company: Dell Glass Company
Years: 1930s – 1940s
Colors: amber, amethyst, blue, crystal, green
Items: 17+

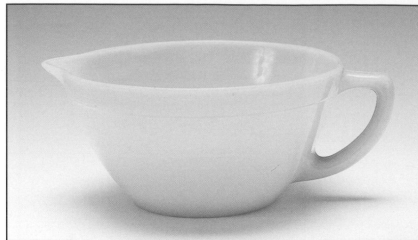

PATTERN NAME: TURQUOISE BLUE,
                              LINE #4000
Company: Anchor Hocking
              Glass Company
Years: 1956 – 1958
Colors: turquoise; Line #4000 also
              comes in red, white
Items: 30

PATTERN NAME: TWIST, BLANK #1252
Company: A.H. Heisey & Company
Years: 1927
Colors: pink, green, marigold, yellow,
              alexandrite
Items: 67

PATTERN NAME: TWISTED OPTIC
Company: Imperial Glass Company
Years: 1927 – 1930
Colors: pink, green, amber, blue,
              yellow
Items: 35+

PATTERN NAME: U.S. SWIRL
Company: U.S. Glass Company
Years: late 1920s
Colors: pink, green, iridescent, crystal
Items: 19

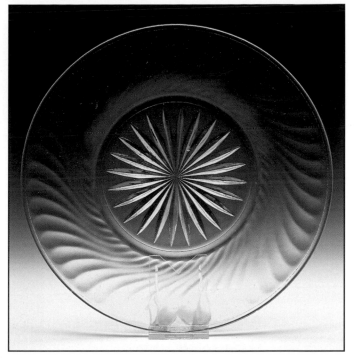

PATTERN NAME: VALENCIA (3500 LINE SHOWN)
Company: The Cambridge Glass Company
Years: 1933 – 1940s
Colors: crystal, pink, blue
Items: 76+

PATTERN NAME: VERLYS PINE CONES
Company: A.H. Heisey & Company
Years: 1950s
Colors: crystal, zircon
Items: 19

PATTERN NAME: VERNON, ETCH #277
Company: Fostoria Glass Company
Years: 1927 – 1934
Colors: green, orchid, amber, azure
Items: 68

PATTERN NAME: "VERNON," #616
Company: Indiana Glass Company
Years: 1930 – 1932
Colors: green, crystal, yellow
Items: 7

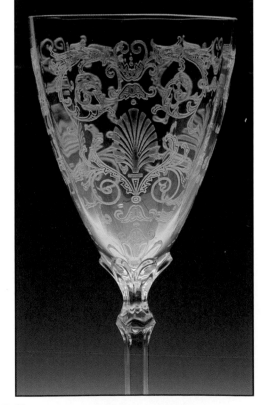

PATTERN NAME: VERSAILLES, ETCH #278, STEM #5098
Company: Fostoria Glass Company
Years: 1928 – 1943
Colors: azure, yellow, pink, green
Items: 90

PATTERN NAME: VESPER,
              ETCH #275
Company: Fostoria Glass
         Company
Years: 1926 – 1934
Colors: amber, blue, green
Items: 83

PATTERN NAME: VICTORIAN; AMERICANA WAFFLE, #1425
Company: A.H. Heisey & Company; Imperial
Years: 1933 – 1953, 1964
Colors: crystal, yellow, cobalt, zircon
Items: 49

PATTERN NAME: VICTORY
Company: Diamond Glass Company
Years: 1929 – 1932
Colors: amber, pink, green,
         cobalt, blue, black
Items: 24

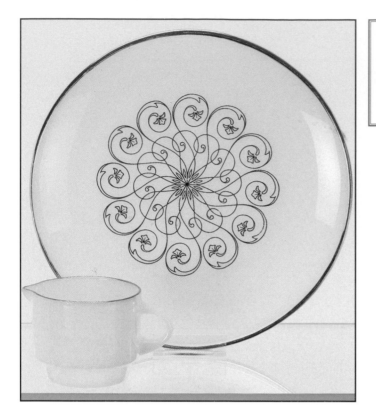

PATTERN NAME: VIENNA LACE
Company: Anchor Hocking Glass Company
Years: 1972 – 1976
Colors: white with decal
Items: 10

PATTERN NAME: VINTAGE, #204
                (VINE & GRAPES)
Company: Fostoria Glass Company
Years: 1904 – 1928
Colors: crystal
Items: 208

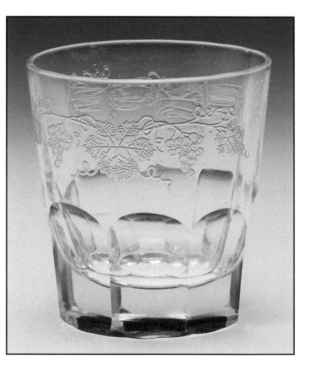

PATTERN NAME: VIRGINIA #267
Company: Fostoria Glass Company
Years: 1923 – 1929
Colors: crystal
Items: 79

PATTERN NAME: VIRGINIA #14184
Company: Tiffin Glass Company
Years: 1920 – mid-1930s
Colors: crystal
Items: 13+

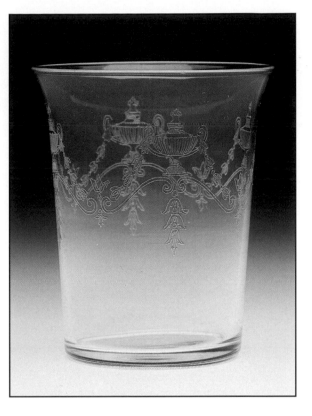

PATTERN NAME: VIRGINIA, CUT FLORAL
(WREATH AND DESIGN)
Company: McKee Glass Company
Years: 1912 – 1924
Colors: crystal
Items: 13

PATTERN NAME: VITROCK
Company: Hocking Glass Company
Years: 1934 – 1937
Colors: white; white with fired-on
              red, green, or yellow
Items: 14

PATTERN NAME: VOGUE #2106
Company: Fostoria Glass Company
Years: 1916 – 1929
Colors: crystal
Items: 90+

PATTERN NAME: WAKEFIELD
Company: Westmoreland Glass
Company
Years: 1930s – 1970s
Colors: crystal, crystal with red
Items: 60

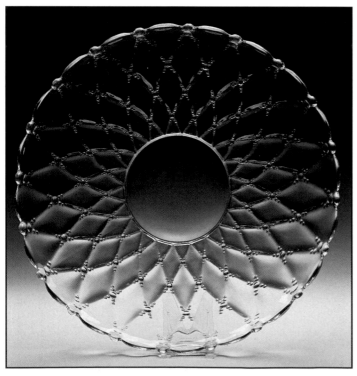

PATTERN NAME: WAMPUM, #1533
Company: A.H. Heisey & Company
Years: 1942
Colors: crystal
Items: 7+

PATTERN NAME: WATER LILIES
                             &CATTAILS
Company: Fenton Art
               Glass Company
Years: 1920s – 1930s
Colors: crystal, opalescent
               green, opalescent
               blue, opalescent
               amethyst
Items: 12

PATTERN NAME: WATERFORD
Company: Hocking Glass Company
Years: 1938 – 1944
Colors: crystal, pink, yellow,
               white, forest green
Items: 32

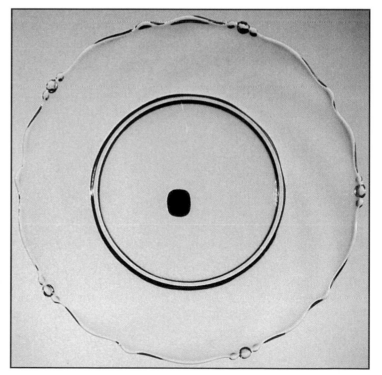

PATTERN NAME: WAVERLY, BLANK #1519
Company: A.H. Heisey & Company
Years: 1949 – 1957
Colors: crystal, amber
Items: 60+

PATTERN NAME: WEDDING RING,
　　　　　　DESIGN #626
Company:　Fostoria Glass Company
Years:　　　1953 – 1975
Colors:　　crystal with silver
Items:　　　15+

PATTERN NAME: WHEAT
Company:　Anchor Hocking Glass Company
Years:　　　1962 – 1966
Colors:　　white with decal
Items:　　　29

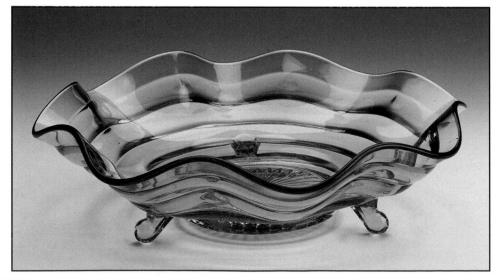

PATTERN NAME: WIDE RIB
　　　　　　LINE #100
Company:　Fenton Art
　　　　　　Glass Company
Years:　　　1920s – 1930s
Colors:　　pink, amber,
　　　　　　green
Items:　　　1

PATTERN NAME: WILDFLOWER
Company: The Cambridge Glass Company
Years: 1935 – 1950s
Colors: crystal, yellow, green, amber, crystal with gold
Items: 85+

PATTERN NAME: WILDFLOWER, ETCH #308
Company: Fostoria Glass Company
Years: 1931 – 1933
Colors: amber, green
Items: 32

PATTERN NAME: WILD ROSE WITH LEAVES
Company: Indiana Glass Company
Years: 1940 – 1980s
Colors: crystal, crystal with tinted green, yellow, pink, amber, satin, flashed colors, white
Items: 7

PATTERN NAME: WILLOW, #335
Company: Fostoria Glass Company
Years: 1939 – 1945
Colors: crystal
Items: 46

PATTERN NAME: WILLOWMERE ETCH #333
Company: Fostoria Glass Company
Years: 1939 – 1971
Colors: crystal
Items: 73

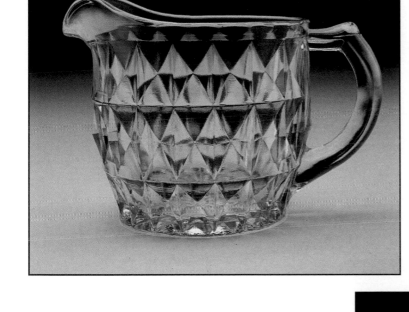

PATTERN NAME: WINDSOR
Company: Jeannette Glass Company
Years: 1936 – 1946
Colors: pink, green, crystal, delphite,
            amberina red, ice blue
Items: 37

PATTERN NAME: WINGS, LINE #100
Company: Westmoreland Glass Company
Years: 1926 – ca. 1938
Colors: crystal, crystal with black
Items: 2

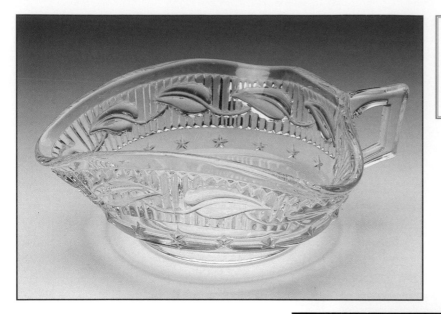

PATTERN NAME: WISTAR, LINE #2620
Company: Fostoria Glass Company
Years: 1941 – 1944
Colors: crystal
Items: 20+

PATTERN NAME: XAVIER, CUT 1100
Company: Standard Glass Company
Years: 1926
Colors: pink, crystal, yellow
Items: 36

PATTERN NAME: YE OLDE IVY, PRISTINE LINE
#3112 STEM
Company: The Cambridge Glass Company
Years: 1935
Colors: crystal, crystal with gold
Items: 20+

PATTERN NAME: YEOMAN
Company: A.H. Heisey & Company
Years: 1915
Colors: pink, green, crystal, yellow, orchid, amber, cobalt
Items: 84

PATTERN NAME: YORKTOWN
Company: Federal Glass Company
Years: 1950s
Colors: crystal, white, amber, iridized
Items: 19

BIBLIOGRAPHY

Archer, Margaret and Douglas. *Imperial Glass*. Paducah, KY: Collector Books, 1978.

Barnett, Jerry. *Paden City, The Color Company*. Astoria, IL: Stevens Publishing Company, 1978.

Bickenheuser, Fred. *Tiffin Glassmasters*. Grove City, OH: Glassmasters Publication, 1979.

———. *Tiffin Glassmasters, II*. Grove City, OH: Glassmasters Publication, 1981.

———. *Tiffin Glassmasters, III*. Grove City, OH: Glassmasters Publication, 1985.

Bones, Frances. *The Book of Duncan Glass*. Des Moines, IA: Wallace-Homestead Co., 1973.

Bredehoft, Neila and Tom. *Hobbs, Brockunier & Co., Glass*. Paducah, KY: Collector Books, 1997.

———. *The Collector's Encyclopedia of Heisey Glass, 1925 – 1938*. Paducah, KY: Collector Books, 1993.

Breeze, George & Linda. *Mysteries of the Moon & Star*. Paducah, KY: Image Graphics, Inc.

Burns, Mary Louise. *Heisey's Glassware of Distinction*. Mesa, AZ: Triangle Books, 1974.

Canton Glass Company, Inc. *Glassware by Canton*. Marion, IN: Canton Glass Company, 1954.

Conder, Lyle, Ed. *Collector's Guide to Heisey's Glassware for Your Table*. Glass City, IN: L.W. Book Sales, 1984.

Duncan & Miller Glass Co. *Hand-Made Duncan, Catalogue No. 89 (Reprint)*. Washington, PA: Duncan & Miller Co., copyright pending by Richard Harold and Robert Roach.

Duncan & Miller, Inc. *Hand-made Duncan, Catalogue No. 93*. Tiffin, OH: Duncan & Miller Division, U.S. Glass, Company, Inc.

Edwards, Bill. *Standard Encyclopedia of Opalescent Glass*. Paducah, KY: Collector Books, 1995.

Emanuele, Concetta, *Stems*. Sunol, CA: Olive Tree Publications, 1970.

Federal Glass Co. *Federal Glassware – Quality You Can See, Catalog No. 56*. Columbus, OH: Federal Glass Co.

Florence, Gene. *Elegant Glassware of the Depression Era, 7th Ed*. Paducah, KY: Collector Books, 1997.

———. *Collector's Encyclopedia of Depression Glass, 13th Ed*. Paducah, KY: Collector Books, 1998.

———. *Stemware Identification, 1920s – 1960s*. Paducah, KY: Collector Books, 1997.

———. *Collectible Glassware of the 40s, 50s, 60s, 4th Ed*. Paducah, KY: Collector Books, 1998.

———. *Anchor Hocking's Fire-King and More*. Paducah, KY: Collector Books, 1998.

Gallagher, Jerry. *A Handbook of Old Morgantown Glass, Vol. 1*. Minneapolis, MN: Merit Printing, 1995.

H.C. Fry Glass Society. *The Collector's Encyclopedia of Fry Glassware*. Paducah, KY: Collector Books, 1990.

Heacock, William. *Encyclopedia of Victorian Colored Pattern Glass*. Marietta, OH: Antiques Publications, 1974.

———. *Opalescent Glass from A to Z*. Marietta, OH: Richardson Printing Corp. 1975.

———. *The Glass Collector, ISS. 2*. Marietta, OH: Peacock Publications, 1982.

———. *The Glass Collector, ISS. 3*. Marietta, OH: Peacock Publications, 1982.

———. *The Glass Collector, ISS. 4*. Marietta, OH: Peacock Publications, 1982.

———. *The Glass Collector, ISS. 6*. Marietta, OH: Peacock Publications, 1983.

———. *Fenton Glass, The First Twenty-Five Years*. Marietta, OH: Richardson Printing, 1978.

———. *Fenton Glass, The Second Twenty-Five Years*. Marietta, OH: O-Val Advertising Corp., 1980.

Hemminger, Ruth, Ed Goshe and Leslie Pina. *Tiffin Modern, Mid Century Art Glass*. Atglen, PA: Schiffer Publishing Ltd., 1997.

Kerr, Ann. *Fostoria, Vol. II*. Paducah, KY: Collector Books, 1997.

King, W.L. *Duncan & Miller Glass, Sec. Ed*. Venetia, PA: Victoria House Museum.

Krause, Gail. *The Encyclopedia of Duncan Glass*. Hicksville, NY: Exposition Press, 1976.

McGrain, Patrick, Ed. *Fostoria, The Popular Years*. Frederick, MD: McGrain Publications, 1983.

Measell, James. *New Martinsville Glass, 1900 – 1944*. Marietta, OH: Antique Publications, 1994.

———. *Fenton Glass, The 1980s Decade*. Marietta, OH: Glass Press, Inc. 1996.

———. *Imperial Glass Encyclopedia, Vol. II*. Marietta, OH: The Glass Press, Inc. 1997.

Miller, Everett R. and Addie R. *The New Martinsville Glass Story Book II, 1920 – 1950*. Manchester, MI, Rymack Printing Company, 1975.

Nat'l Cambridge Collectors, Inc. *Genuine Handmade Cambridge, 1949 – 1953*. Paducah, KY: Collector Books, 1978.

———. *The Cambridge Glass Co., 1930 – 1934*. Paducah, KY: Collector Books, 1976.

National Greentown Glass Assoc. *The D.C. Jenkins Glass Company Catalog*, Hillsdale, MI: Ferguson Communications, 1984.

Newark Heisey Collectors Club, *Heisey by Imperial and Imperial Glass by Lenox*. Newark, OH: Heisey Collectors of America, Inc. 1980.

Nye, Mark. *Cambridge Stemware, Sec. Ed.* Brooklyn, MI: Mark A. Nye, 1994.

Page, Bob and Dale Frederiksen. *A Collection of American Crystal*. Greensboro, NC: Page-Frederiksen Publishing Company, 1995.

———. *Tiffin is Forever*. Greensboro, NC: Page-Frederiksen Publishing Co., 1994.

Pina, Leslie. *Fostoria... 1887 – 1986*. Atglen, PA: Schiffer Publishing Ltd., 1995.

Ream, Louise, Neila M., and Thomas H. Bredehoft. *Encyclopedia of Heisey Glassware, Vol. 1*. Newark, OH: Heisey Collectors of America, Inc., 1977.

Sferrazza, Julie. *Farber Brothers, Krome Kraft*. Marietta, OH: Antique Publications, 1988.

Stout, Sandra McPhee. *The Complete Book of McKee*. N . Kansas City, KS: The Trojan Press, 1972.

———. *Depression Glass, Number One*. Des Moines, IA: Wallace-Homestead, 1970.

———. *Depression Glass, Number Two*. Des Moines, IA: Wallace-Homestead, 1971.

———. *Heisey on Parade*. Lombard, IL: Wallace-Homestead, 1985.

Viking Glass Company. *Treasured American Glass*. New Martinsville, WV: Viking Glass Company.

Vogel, Clarence W. *Heisey's First Ten Years...1896 – 1905*. Plymouth, OH: Heisey Publications, 1969.

———. *Heisey's Colonial Years...1906 – 1922*. Plymouth, OH: Heisey Publications, 1969.

———. *Heisey's Art and Colored Glass, 1922 – 1942*. Plymouth, OH: Heisey Publications, 1970.

———. *Heisey's Early and Late Years, 1896 – 1958*. Plymouth, OH: Heisey Publications, 1971.

Weatherman, Hazel Marie. *Colored Glassware of the Depression Era 2*. Springfield, MO: Weatherman Glassbooks, 1974.

———. *Fostoria, Its First Fifty Years*. Springfield, MO: The Weathermans, 1979.

Welker, Mary, Lyle and Lynn. *The Cambridge Glass Co.* Newark, OH: Spencer Walker Press, 1974.

Whitmyer, Margaret & Kenn. *Fenton Art Glass, 1907 – 1939*. Paducah, KY: Collector Books, 1996.

Wilson, Charles West. *Westmoreland Glass*. Paducah, KY: Collector Books, 1996.

Wilson, Jack D. *Phoenix and Consolidated Art Glass: 1926 – 1980*. Marietta, OH: Antique Publications, 1996.

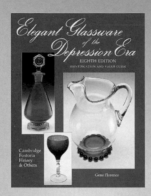

Other books on glassware by Gene Florence

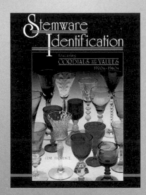

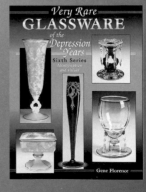

From top, clockwise on facing page:

Collector's Encyclopedia of Depression Glass $19.95
Anchor Hocking's Fire-King and More $24.95
Collectible Glassware from the 40s, 50s , 60s $19.95
Pocket Guide to Depression Glass $9.95
Elegant Glassware of the Depression Era $19.95
Kitchen Glassware of the Depression Years $19.95
Stemware Identification $24.95
Very Rare Glassware of the Depression Years, Third Series $24.95
Very Rare Glassware of the Depression Years, Fifth Series $24.95
Very Rare Glassware of the Depression Years, Sixth Series $24.95

Other books by Gene Florence not pictured:

Collector's Encyclopedia of Occupied Japan I $14.95
Collector's Encyclopedia of Occupied Japan II $14.95
Collector's Encyclopedia of Occupied Japan III $14.95
Collector's Encyclopedia of Occupied Japan IV $14.95
Collector's Encyclopedia of Occupied Japan V $14.95
Occupied Japan Price Guides I – V $9.95

Copies of these books may be ordered from:

Gene Florence	or	**Collector Books**
P.O. Box 22186	P.O. Box 64	P.O. Box 3009
Lexington, KY 40522	Astatula, FL 34705	Paducah, KY 42002-3009

Add $2.00 postage for the first book, 30¢ for each additional book.

Schroeder's
ANTIQUES
Price Guide

. . . is the #1 best-selling antiques & collectibles value guide on the market today, and here's why . . .

Schroeder's ANTIQUES Price Guide

OUR #1 BEST SELLER!

Identification & Values Of Over 50,000 Antiques & Collectibles

8½ x 11, 608 Pages, $12.95

COLLECTOR BOOKS
A Division of Schroeder Publishing Co., Inc.